After the Rainbow Bridge

Managing the Grief of Pet Loss

Tonya M. Pierce

Table of Contents

Introduction

Ever noticed that quiet tug at your heart when you see someone walking their dog or when you hear a playful meow echo down the hallway of an apartment building? That feeling? That's the echo of a connection—a unique and powerful bond that forms between humans and their furry companions. It's a companionship created from love, loyalty, and a silent understanding that cannot be described in words. But this beautiful story of shared lives and love also holds a reality we all must face: the inevitable goodbye that comes with losing our animal friends.

The loss can be a shattering blow for those who have opened their hearts and homes to a pet. It can feel like the very foundation of your world has crumbled, leaving a gaping hole that seems impossible to fill. This grief is often misunderstood and dismissed by some as trivial or unimportant. But anyone who's ever looked into the soulful eyes of a devoted pet—anyone who's felt the unconditional love radiating from a wagging tail or a gentle purr—knows this grief is far from insignificant. It's a deep, raw pain that can leave you feeling lost and adrift.

I know this feeling all too well. I have lost not one, but two of my cherished companions, and the pain that followed was a storm of emotions. It was a wave of indescribable grief, a hollowness that settled deep within. But grief, however heavy it is, isn't the end of the story.

To be honest, the words within this book aren't here to tell you how to get over your pet's death quickly. They're not here to minimize your feelings or to tell you your emotions are silly or unimportant. We all grieve differently, and there's no one-size-fits-all approach to healing. What I can tell you, however, is that you will find a space of understanding and empathy within these pages.

As a fellow pet owner who has lost more than just my pets—more than words can define—it's important to shatter the myth that pet-loss grief is somehow lesser than other kinds of grief and is somehow undeserving of genuine sorrow. It is not something to be hidden away because of unempathetic eyes or hearts. Pet loss and grief are valid experiences that make us human.

Here, in these pages, we honor the depth of your grief. We acknowledge it as a valid and significant experience, akin to losing a cherished family member. Apart from mine, you'll find real stories, shared by people who have walked this same path of loss. They'll tell you about the pain, the emptiness, and the tears that wouldn't stop flowing. But they'll also tell you about the healing, the moments of unexpected joy amid the sorrow, and the enduring love that continues to connect them to their furry companions even after they're gone.

These stories pay tribute to the strength of the bond we share with our pets. They're a reminder that even in the darkest moments of despair, there is still light. There's the light of shared memories, the warmth of love that continues to radiate, and the hope that, as you move through your healing, you'll find a way to carry that love with you, forever a part of your story.

So, turn the page and we can embark on this journey together. We'll create a space for your tears, for your anger, and for your laughter as you remember the good times. We'll explore ways to navigate the pain and find solace in the memories. We'll help you honor the unique connection you shared with your pet and discover how that love can continue to guide you, even in their absence. This is a path of healing and self-discovery, of finding a way to live with the loss while cherishing the love that remains.

Chapter 1:

The Unbreakable Connection

Have you ever stopped to think about the special bond between us—humans—and our pets? When you think about it, it's more than just feeding them and taking them for walks—it's a deep, emotional connection that shapes our lives in ways we might not even realize.

It's time to explore that connection and understand why it's so important, especially when we're facing tough times like pet loss and grief.

Exploring the Human–Pet Connection

As a pet owner, you must have noticed your pet behaving in a way that has left you surprised. For example, think of times when you were feeling down, maybe even a little lonely. Then your furry friend comes bounding over, tail wagging and eyes full of love—it's a very common experience, but have you ever wondered why? It's like they just know how to make everything better, right? Even if they can't speak, you understand them perfectly.

Well, research has shown that pets have this amazing ability to sense our emotions and respond with love and comfort. It's like they're our therapists, always there to lift our spirits and make us feel loved (Robinson & Segal, 2019).

So, what exactly is this human–pet connection all about? Simply put, it's the deep emotional bond that exists between pets and people. It's the feeling of joy you get when your dog greets you at the door or the sense of calm that washes over you when your cat curls up in your lap. This connection isn't just about companionship—it's about understanding, trust, and unconditional love. When you think about your pet, what comes to mind? Maybe it's the way they greet you with enthusiasm after a long day or the way they curl up next to you and purr when you're feeling blue. These moments of connection aren't just fleeting—they're the foundation of a friendship that's built on trust, loyalty, and unconditional love.

Science backs this up, too. When we interact with our pets, our bodies release feel-good hormones like oxytocin and dopamine, which help reduce stress and anxiety. It's no wonder we feel so happy and content when we're with our furry friends. And the best part? This bond only grows stronger over time, as we share more experiences and create lasting memories together (Johns Hopkins Medicine, 2022).

The Wonderful Friendship and Understanding That Pets Provide

Pets have this incredible knack for understanding us in ways that no one else can. They're like silent companions, always there to listen without judgment or expectation. Whether it's a quiet cuddle on the couch or a playful romp in the park, these moments of companionship are what make our bond with our pets so special.

But the benefits of this connection go beyond warm fuzzies and happy memories.

Whether it's going for a walk or playing fetch in the backyard, having a pet encourages us to get up and get moving, which can improve our overall health and fitness. Pets can also be great conversation starters and help us connect with others who share our love for animals. Plus, owning a pet can nudge us toward more positive habits and keep us away from self-destructive activities and behaviors. When we're feeling down, they can sense our emotions and offer a comforting cuddle or a purr that seems to magically lower our blood pressure. They can chase away loneliness, too, simply by being there and listening, even if they don't quite understand every word.

If you're feeling lost and lacking purpose, pets can be your reason to get up in the morning. Caring for them gives you a sense of accomplishment and responsibility that can be very uplifting. They can even be your best secret-keeper, someone you can talk to without judgment, knowing their love is unconditional. And let's not forget the security some pets provide, making you feel safer when you're feeling vulnerable.

They may not be able to talk, but their love and companionship speak volumes, reminding us that we're never alone on this journey called life.

Pets as Family Members

When you stop to think just how valuable your pet is to you, you'll realize that they're more than just animals we've adopted—they're cherished members of our family. From the moment they come into our lives, they become an integral part of our daily routines, our special moments, and our hearts.

Pets become essential members of the family unit, providing joy, companionship, and a sense of belonging. They're there to celebrate our victories and comfort us during our struggles. They offer unconditional love and support, no matter what life throws our way. Just the same as a parent or a sibling, their presence gives us one simple thought—home.

Aside from the emotional aspect, pets also enrich our lives by being our constant companions, always there to greet us with a wagging tail or a soft purr. They:

- Provide comfort and emotional support during times of stress or sadness.

- Encourage us to be more active and enjoy the outdoors through walks, hikes, and playtime.

- Teach us valuable lessons about responsibility, empathy, and unconditional love.

- Offer companionship for people of all ages, from children to seniors, helping to combat loneliness and isolation.

At the end of the day, our pets aren't just animals—they're family, bringing joy, laughter, and love into our lives each and every day.

The Role of Pets in Our Lives

So, they're family members and our loyal companions, but have you wondered about the roles that our pets play in our lives? It's fascinating to consider just how much they contribute to our well-being and happiness.

How Pets Can Bring Comfort and Emotional Support

Our pets have this incredible ability to comfort us during tough times, sometimes in ways we don't even notice. It's like they can sense how we're feeling—almost like they have a built-in empathy meter. Dogs, for instance, are great at picking up on tiny changes in our body language, voice, or even our smell. They can tell when we're stressed or sad. And when they pick up on this, they often come over and offer some gentle affection to show they care. These simple gestures can be incredibly calming, helping to ease our anxiety and stress.

Think about it. When you're feeling overwhelmed or alone, just having your pet nearby can make a big difference. Their presence is a kind of quiet reassurance, a reminder that you're not going through this alone. Whether it's a purring cat curled up on your lap or a dog resting its head on your knee, that simple connection can feel incredibly grounding and supportive.

Pets can also be a great distraction from worries and anxieties. Sometimes, all you need is a break from your thoughts, and playing fetch in the backyard, going for a walk, or even just snuggling on the couch with your furry friend can do wonders. Their playful energy and enthusiasm can lift your spirits and remind you to find joy in the little things.

In short, pets offer comfort and emotional support in several ways. Their empathy, their companionship, and their ability to distract us are all incredibly valuable. These gentle creatures play a vital role in helping us cope with life's challenges, and their presence can be a source of immense strength and solace, especially during times of grief.

My Story

At the end of a long, awful day at work, with deadlines, meetings, and endless things to do, I left the office feeling totally drained. The commute home was even worse; the subway trip was a nightmare. More than an hour later than my usual time getting back, I finally dragged myself through the door, defeated and exhausted. The not-so-surprising part was how I was met by Simon's excited bark and that wagging tail of his. It felt like he knew exactly how awful I felt. Ignoring the usual boundless energy he had after my day at work, he took on the role of a stress reliever and showered me with affection, his eyes full of love.

Sinking onto the couch, I felt the stress melt away as he snuggled in beside me, his soft fur like a warm hug. Stroking his fur, I could feel my tension drain away. Simon was like a magic stress reliever, reminding me I wasn't alone in this crazy world.

We spent the rest of the evening together, his calming presence working its magic. A walk around the neighborhood, some fresh air, and with Simon by my side, the worries of the day faded away. By bedtime, I felt refreshed and ready to tackle whatever tomorrow threw my way. As I drifted off to sleep, Simon curled up at my side, a comforting reminder that no matter what, he'd always be there. I can think of no better emotional support than that.

Emotional Connections Beyond Words

Let's take a short detour with one question: Have you ever experienced a deep, emotional connection with someone without exchanging a single word? It's a phenomenon that goes beyond language and relies on the power of empathy, intuition, and love. Just as humans can connect on a profound level without speaking, so, too, can we connect with our beloved pets.

Love has a way of bridging the gap between words and understanding. When we truly love someone—whether it's a friend, family member, or pet—we become attuned to their emotions, thoughts, and needs. We can sense when they're happy, sad, or in need of comfort, even without them saying a word.

This same principle applies to the bond between pets and their owners. Pets are incredibly intuitive creatures, capable of picking up on subtle cues and emotions that we may not even be aware of ourselves. They can sense when we're feeling stressed, anxious, or upset, and they respond with steadfast loyalty and support. Just as I mentioned in my story, my dog was able to sense what I was experiencing without the need for shared words.

Through unstated communication, pets and their owners form a deep, emotional bond that goes beyond words. It's a bond built on trust, understanding, and unconditional love. Whether it's a comforting nuzzle, a sympathetic gaze, or a gentle paw on our hand, pets have a unique way of letting us know that they're there for us, no matter what.

So, the emotional connection between pets and their owners pays tribute to the power of love and empathy. It's a bond that transcends language and defies explanation, yet it's one of the most meaningful connections we can experience in life.

How Pets Intuitively Detect Their Human Counterparts' Emotions

Pets, particularly dogs, have a remarkable ability to intuitively detect their human counterparts' emotions. It's as if they have a sixth sense for understanding our feelings, often picking up on subtle cues.

One way that pets detect our emotions is through our body language. Dogs, in particular, are highly attuned to changes in our posture, facial expressions, and tone of voice. They can sense when we're feeling happy, sad, anxious, or stressed, and they respond accordingly. For example, if you're feeling down, your dog might approach you with a comforting nuzzle or a gentle paw on the leg. This is to offer you solace and support.

Pets are also good at reading the energy and atmosphere of their environment. They can sense tension in the air and can become anxious or agitated in response. When the energy is calm and positive, pets are more likely to be relaxed and content.

Another factor that contributes to pets' ability to detect human emotions is their keen sense of smell. Dogs have an incredibly sensitive sense of smell, capable of detecting subtle changes in our scent that may be associated with different emotional states. This heightened olfactory sense allows them to pick up on chemical signals known as *pheromones*, which are released in response to various emotions.

Then, too, the bond between pets and their humans plays a significant role in their ability to detect emotions. Through years of companionship and shared experiences, pets become attuned to our moods, preferences, and behaviors. They learn to anticipate our needs and respond accordingly, offering comfort and support when we need it most. They have emotions just the same as us.

Sources of Joy

Our furry friends bring so much sunshine into our lives. They fill our hearts in all sorts of ways.

Emotionally, they shower us with unconditional love and are always there for us, no matter what. Their happy greetings after a long day or a snuggle on the couch can instantly lift our spirits. It's a warm, fuzzy feeling you just can't get anywhere else.

Physically, they keep us moving. Dogs in particular need regular walks or playtime. These walks benefit both of us. They stay healthy, and we get some exercise to help us de-stress and feel better overall. Taking care of them, from feeding to grooming, gives us a sense of purpose and accomplishment, too.

Mentally, pets are amazing stress relievers. Spending time with them can lower our stress hormones and boost our happy hormones. They also provide a sense of routine and stability, which can be especially helpful when we're feeling down.

One memory I'll always cherish is a walk I took with my dog Simon. We explored nature together, just the two of us. Seeing his boundless energy and playful spirit was a joyful reminder of the simple things in life. Pets have that special way of spreading happiness and laughter wherever they go, whether it's chasing a ball or just curling up beside us. It's the joy that comes from living life to the fullest.

The Healing Power of Pet Companionship

The bond between us and our pets is surprisingly powerful, especially when we're hurting. It all stems from that deep connection we share. This connection helps heal us in so many ways, especially after losing a furry friend.

Pets are amazing comforters. Their unconditional love and loyalty feel like a warm hug, easing the pain of grief and helping us heal emotionally. Just petting them can release happy chemicals in our brains, making us feel calmer and better.

They also bring a sense of routine and stability into our lives, which can be comforting during tough times. Feeding them and playing together all create a purpose that can be grounding. Plus, they're great at making us laugh and forget about our worries for a while, which is especially helpful when we're grieving.

Along with the many emotional benefits, pets can even improve our physical health! Studies show they can lower our blood pressure and stress, making us feel better overall. They also get us moving, whether it's going on walks or enjoying playtime, which is good for our bodies and minds, especially when we're dealing with grief.

The bottom line? The healing power of pets comes from the special bond we share with them. They comfort us, support us, and love us unconditionally. As we explore healing in this book, we'll see how this amazing bond helps us navigate grief, find strength, and honor the memory of our furry companions.

Emotional Health and Well-Being

It's our furry friends to the rescue by boosting our emotional health and happiness. They're like little therapists with fur, feathers, or scales, lifting our spirits when we're down and offering a warm, fuzzy hug or a playful game of fetch whenever we need it. The special bond between humans and pets plays a huge role in keeping our minds and emotions healthy.

The Feel-Good Power of Pets

Having a pet by your side has long been known to be good for your mental health. They chase away loneliness, depression, and anxiety with their unconditional love and happy vibes. Feeling stressed? Just petting your furry friend can lower your stress levels and help you relax. Plus, taking care of a pet gives you a sense of purpose and routine, which can be especially helpful if you're feeling down.

Science Says So, Too

All sorts of studies are finding tons of benefits to having a pet. From feeling less lonely and depressed to just having a generally better mood, the evidence is clear: Pets are amazing for our emotional well-being (Martins et al., 2023). This research shows how important the human-animal bond is—not just for kids, but for people of all ages and backgrounds.

Finding Comfort in Grief

Pets as Furry Therapists

We all know pets can be a joy, but they become superheroes during tough times, especially when we're grieving a loss. It's like they have a sixth sense for our sadness. No matter what, they're there to offer their never-ending love and support.

A gentle nudge with their nose, a rumbling purr, or just curling up by our side—pets have a way of making us feel understood and not alone, even in the darkest of times. Here's a story that shows their amazing power:

A Cat's Comfort

Imagine losing your daughter, especially someone as special as a 23-year-old with Down syndrome. That's what one woman went through. In the crushing grief, her outdoor cat, usually independent, surprised everyone. The cat started acting differently, sensing her distress. It would sit with her all day, sleep at her feet at night, and keep a watchful eye on her. This unexpected companionship became a source of comfort and helped her heal faster.

This story, and countless others like it, highlights the immeasurable impact pets have on our ability to navigate grief. They offer comfort and become anchors during times of sadness and loss. By sharing these real-life experiences, we want to showcase the extraordinary bond between humans and pets. We'll see just how powerful pets are in helping us cope with life's challenges and find solace in moments of need.

*****

Pets are more than just animals; they are living beings with souls as well as hearts and bodies, just like us. The only difference is that they cannot speak, but their actions and behaviors communicate better than words. Our pets are more than creatures or wild beasts; they're family. They are a source of love and joy, fueling that unbreakable connection.

As we move to the next chapter, we'll go deeper into the complexities of grief following the loss of a beloved pet, providing reassurance and understanding while acknowledging the intensity of emotions experienced during this difficult time.

Chapter 2:

Your Grief Is Valid

Losing a beloved pet can be an incredibly challenging and emotional experience. It can leave you stuck, in a place that can only be described as limbo. But this isn't a place that you need to be trapped in while hiding from the world. Grief is a journey. And with time and healing, you will find closure.

In this chapter, we look into the importance of acknowledging your emotions as you work through the intensity of feelings following the loss of your pet.

The Importance of Acknowledging Your Emotions

At times, it can be tempting to suppress or ignore our emotions, especially when they feel overwhelming. However, acknowledging and honoring our feelings is a crucial step in the healing process. By allowing ourselves to feel and express our emotions, we open the door to healing and self-discovery.

Then again, just because something is going to benefit us doesn't mean that we feel motivated to embrace it. With grief, there will be times when you barely have the will to move forward. But this is entirely normal.

The Overwhelming Effect of Pet Loss

Losing a cherished pet can have a huge emotional impact, leaving us feeling overwhelmed by a range of intense emotions. From intense sadness and emptiness to feelings of guilt and regret, the grieving process can be all-encompassing.

This is the beginning of grief; by acknowledging the depth and complexity of these emotions, we can begin to navigate the grieving process with compassion and self-awareness. Through self-reflection and self-compassion, we can learn to honor our feelings and find solace in the memories of our beloved pets. You need to understand that this is a natural response to loss. Pet-loss grief isn't an exaggeration.

The Turbulence of Grief

The grieving process is often likened to a turbulent rollercoaster ride, filled with ups and downs, twists and turns. At times, we may find ourselves engulfed in waves of intense emotion, while at other times, we might experience moments of calm and clarity. It's important to recognize that grief is not a linear journey but, rather, a complex and ever-changing process.

Then, too, as we work through our grief, it's important to permit ourselves to feel whatever emotions arise, without judgment or self-criticism. Because, by allowing ourselves to experience the full range of emotions associated with grief, we can begin to process our feelings and move toward healing.

Reflecting on the Unpredictable Nature of Grieving

Grief is a deeply personal and unpredictable process, characterized by a whirlwind of emotions that can ebb and flow without warning. At times, we may find ourselves consumed by sadness, overwhelmed by the weight of our loss. At other times, we may experience fleeting rushes of longing, as memories of our beloved pet come flooding back.

The intensity and duration of these emotions can vary greatly from person to person—even from moment to moment. What might feel unbearable one day could feel more manageable the next, only to resurface with unexpected intensity at a later time.

In this unpredictability, it's important to be gentle with ourselves and to allow ourselves the space and time to grieve in our way. There is no right or wrong way to grieve, and it's okay to experience a wide range of emotions as we navigate the grieving process.

Recognizing the Spectrum of Feelings

Losing a beloved pet can unleash a wide range of emotions, each valid and deserving of acknowledgment. And, grieving for a pet doesn't make you weak; in fact, it's a very normal human experience.

To be honest, when we lose a beloved pet, it's normal to feel a rollercoaster of emotions. But you know what? It's important to let yourself feel and process these emotions; it's how we truly honor the special bond we share with our furry companions.

I remember when my dogs passed away. The sadness felt like a heavy weight on my chest. Some days, it was hard to even get out of bed. But as tough as it was, I had to give myself space to mourn and feel that pain deeply. It was a way of acknowledging just how much they meant to me.

It's also common to feel a sense of shame or worry about how others might perceive your grief. But your bond with your pet was unique and special, and your feelings are valid. Don't let anyone diminish that. The road ahead might feel daunting, but you don't have to walk it alone. Lean on your loved ones, find supportive communities, and be gentle with yourself. Healing takes time, and by processing these complex emotions, you're honoring your pet's memory in the most beautiful way possible.

So, take a deep breath, my friend. Your feelings are normal, and you have the strength to get through this one step at a time. Your furry companion will forever hold a special place in your heart, and that love will guide you toward brighter days ahead.

Letting Yourself Feel by Embracing Your Emotional Journey

In grief, it's natural to experience a whirlwind of emotions, and while they may feel overwhelming at times, it's important to remember that they are an essential part of the healing process. Why? Well, validation of our emotions is crucial in the grieving process.

Suppressing emotions can have detrimental effects on our mental and emotional well-being. When we bury our feelings, rather than allow ourselves to express them, they can fester and manifest in unhealthy ways, such as physical symptoms, increased anxiety, or prolonged depression (WebMD Editorial Contributors, 2024). By permitting ourselves to grieve fully, we create space for healing and growth.

Finding Healthy Outlets for Your Emotions

Our general well-being depends on having constructive outlets for our emotions. We can grieve more easily if we find methods to express and process our feelings. Here are a few examples of healthy outlets for grief:

- **Journaling:** Writing down your thoughts and feelings can be a powerful way to process your emotions and gain clarity about your experience.

- **Talking to a friend or counselor:** Sharing your feelings with a trusted confidante or professional can provide validation and support as you navigate the grieving process.

- **Engaging in creative activities:** Activities like painting, drawing, or playing music can offer a therapeutic outlet for expressing emotions and finding solace in creativity.

- **Spending time in nature:** Connecting with nature can provide a sense of peace and perspective, allowing you to find comfort and solace in the beauty of the world around you.

By creating healthy outlets for your emotions and accepting how you feel, you can grieve with bravery and fortitude, paying tribute to your cherished pet's memory along the way.

Dealing With Self-Blame and Regret

It is common for pet owners to experience regret and guilt after their pet dies. It is normal to wonder if there was anything more we could have done to spare them from harm or save their life. We might relive specific moments from their dying days, questioning whether we overlooked warning indications or took actions that unintentionally accelerated their decline. If these feelings of guilt and self-blame are not addressed, they can become overwhelming and cause long-term distress. These emotions can be incredibly mentally and emotionally taxing. For this reason, let's explore how to address these challenging emotions with self-compassion and forgiveness as we grieve.

Developing Self-Compassion and Forgiveness

- Develop self-awareness by identifying and addressing feelings of guilt and self-blame when they surface, without passing judgment. Recognize that experiencing these emotions is normal during the grieving process.

- Stop talking badly to yourself. Replace self-blame with self-compassion and with understanding thoughts. Remind yourself that you did the best you could with the information and resources available to you at the time.

- Ask for help. If you need encouragement and affirmation, do not hesitate to ask friends, family, or a therapist. Open communication about your emotions can help put your experience in perspective and lessen the weight of your guilt.

- Practice self-forgiveness by accepting responsibility for any errors or shortfalls you may have seen. Realize that clinging to guilt and self-blame only makes things worse and keeps you from getting better. Rather, decide to let go of the guilt and accept forgiveness as a means of recovery and development.

- Respect the memory of your pet by directing your regret and guilt into constructive activities that pay tribute to their life and legacy. Think about making a memorial, doing volunteer work at an animal shelter, or participating in events that honor the relationship you had with your cherished friend.

Through self-compassion and forgiveness, you can overcome feelings of guilt and self-blame, allowing yourself to grieve more easily and find healing even amid loss.

Instead of getting stuck in that cycle of self-blame, try to be kind to yourself. Remind yourself that you loved your pet fiercely and that your intentions were always pure. They knew how much you cared, and that's what truly matters.

Seeking Compassion and Support From Others

When you're grieving the loss of a beloved pet, it's so important to have a strong support system around you—and that includes being compassionate and supportive toward yourself, too. Let's go over the power of compassion and support during these tough times.

Do you know how deeply Queen Elizabeth II loved her corgis? For decades, those loyal companions were a constant source of joy and comfort for her, through good times and bad. Their unwavering affection and loyalty meant everything, proving that the human-animal bond goes beyond any social status or background. Pets can have such an amazing impact on our lives, no matter who we are.

Then there's the story of John and his lab, Max. Those two were inseparable. Max was far more than just a pet; he was a cherished family member who stuck by John's side through thick and thin. When Max passed away after years of adventures and memories together, John was devastated. But he found solace in reflecting on all the love, laughter, and unbreakable bonds they shared. Max's legacy lived on through the impact he had on John's life.

And then there's Sarah and her beloved cat, Whiskers. Despite facing some tough personal challenges, Sarah always had Whiskers's unconditional love and companionship to lean on. Their bond gave her strength, purpose, and connection when she needed it most. Even though Whiskers is gone now, Sarah carries that love and those special memories deep in her heart, forever grateful for the impact her feline friend had.

As you read these stories, I hope it resonates with your experiences of the beautiful, irreplaceable bonds you have shared with your animal companions. Losing them leaves such a void, but by opening up to support from others who understand and are compassionate with us, we can find solace and healing.

I say this because I know it's true.

My Story

Sophie

It was a Saturday morning, which I remember all too clearly. I was just feeling too drained to give Sophie and Simon their usual grooming. So, I took them to the groomer instead, never imagining anything could go wrong. When I got that call saying Sophie had passed away from some kind of heart issue while there, I was just devastated. I tortured myself, wondering if staying home and grooming them myself could have prevented it. The guilt and self-blame were so heavy, and it took ages for them to lift. But I accepted my grief as a part of the cycle that I had to go through to get the healing I needed to carry on with my life.

Simon

My other dog, Simon, had a different story. First, he seemed to adjust okay as an only pup after losing his lifelong buddy, Sophie. He and I became even closer. Every day after work, I'd come home to his excited barks and energy. He loved our little games of hide-and-seek, always picking the same sneaky spot under my bed to make me hunt for him. But then, one day, I came home to silence. I searched everywhere, finally finding Simon's body in that same beloved hiding spot. A pulmonary embolism had taken him from me, too.

Losing them both was one of the hardest things I've ever gone through. Even now, I can't help but recount all the special memories, how Sophie used to steal Simon's food, how he shadowed her every move. My heart aches, and though the grief is overwhelming at times, having compassion for myself and seeking the support of others who understand helps me keep their love alive.

As I reflect on the love and companionship Sophie and Simon brought into my life, I'm reminded of the tremendous privilege it is to share our lives with pets. Though they may no longer be physically with us, their spirit remains eternally intertwined with ours, guiding us forward with love and remembrance. And while my heart still aches for their presence, I find solace in the possibility of opening my heart to another furry friend, honoring Sophie and Simon's legacies in the process.

Finding Common Ground: Bonding Through Shared Grief

Now, this may seem strange, but our desire to bond with others in good times and bad is intriguing because it can be helpful, particularly when life gets tough. The only possible explanation is that, as social beings, we require the assistance of others in nearly every negative moment or encounter to move forward and make it more memorable. What do I mean by this? All right, consider it. When you tell others about your good fortune or experiences, their happiness makes you feel even better. Finding comfort and understanding in the experiences that others have shared can be extremely reassuring during difficult times. Making connections with people who have also gone through the agony of losing a pet—through a grief support group, an online community, or a supportive friend—can help lessen feelings of loneliness and isolation. In this sense, we honor the relationship we had with our cherished companions by creating a sense of solidarity through telling our stories, listening to others, and showing empathy and support.

We learn that we are not alone in our grief when we connect with others who have also experienced the loss of a pet. These connections provide us with a map to help us navigate the difficult emotions associated with grief. We find comfort in the knowledge that we are not alone in our suffering and validation for our emotions in these shared experiences. We create connections that go beyond words through sincere talks and tears shed together, bound by the love and loss we all bear within.

We experience the purest form of human connection's healing power when we rely on one another for understanding and support. We find the courage to face the grief journey head-on when we are embraced by kind spirits who share our suffering. We pay tribute to our cherished pets' memories together and take solace in the knowledge that their love will always be a valued aspect of our lives.

How to Meet People in Similar Circumstances

Finding support and understanding from others who have also gone through pet loss can be immensely helpful while grieving. To create a friendly and encouraging atmosphere and make connections with people who have gone through similar things, try these methods:

Join Online Pet-Loss Support Groups

People can connect with others going through similar experiences, share their stories, and offer support in a variety of online communities and forums devoted to pet-loss grief. Websites such as PetLoss.com, www.rainbowsbridge.com, and the Pet Loss Support forum on Reddit (https://www.reddit.com/r/Petloss/) offer secure environments where people can express their emotions and obtain understanding and support from one another.

Attend Pet-Loss Support Groups or Workshops

Many local communities offer seminars or support groups tailored specifically for people experiencing the loss of a pet. These groups provide opportunities for face-to-face interaction, experience exchange, and the acquisition of enlightening information and coping skills from other participants and knowledgeable facilitators.

Reach Out to Friends and Family

Even though friends and family might not completely comprehend the depth of grief associated with pet loss, reaching out to them for support can still be consoling. Tell people you love about your feelings honestly and openly, and they will listen to you and be understanding and compassionate in return.

Engage in Online Social Media Communities

On social media platforms like Facebook, Instagram, and X (Twitter), people who have lost pets share their stories, photos, and memories through pet-related groups and hashtags. Interacting with these groups can give you a feeling of community and support from like-minded pet owners who recognize the special relationship that exists between people and animals.

Seek Professional Help

Seeking assistance from a certified therapist or counselor who specializes in pet-loss grief may be wise if feelings of loneliness or bereavement become too much to handle. They can offer a secure, accepting environment where you can explore your feelings, create coping mechanisms, and get individualized support that meets your needs.

Through proactive exploration of helpful communities and resources, you can establish connections with like-minded pet owners who share their experiences of grieving for a pet. You will be greeted with kindness and understanding, and not rejected or condemned.

The Healing Impact of Shared Experiences and Emotions

It can be incredibly healing to share feelings and experiences with people who have also lost a pet. Why? Talking about experiences and feelings with sympathetic people builds empathy and a sense of community, which lessens feelings of loneliness and isolation.

It can help normalize your grief experience to hear about other people's pet losses. Understanding that grief is a natural response to losing a beloved pet helps ease any guilt or shame that may arise from the societal pressure to "get over" the loss quickly.

Interacting with people who have experienced similar losses also helps to develop compassion and empathy. A supportive community fosters a sense of belonging, which can be comforting during trying times.

Healing can also be accelerated by talking about your loss with others and getting their support and validation. Openly and vulnerably expressing your feelings in a secure environment promotes catharsis and emotional release, which in turn promotes healing and, ultimately, acceptance of the loss.

Finding Peace in Memories

Finding peace in treasured memories can be a source of consolation and healing as we travel through the grief journey associated with pet loss. We can honor our beloved pets' lives and find comfort during grief by thinking back on the memorable times we spent with them.

Pause to remember the good times you had with your animal companion. Think back to the times when your relationship was defined by your endless love, laughter, and playful antics. Accept these recollections as a testament to the significant influence your pet had on your life.

Thinking back on treasured memories has therapeutic advantages for recovery. It enables us to recognize the special relationship we had with our pets and the enormous influence they had on our lives. We can take solace in the knowledge that our pets will always have a particular place in our hearts by thinking back on happy and loving times.

*****

Now, as we come to the end of this chapter, remember that it's critical to acknowledge that your grief is real and worthy of sympathy and understanding. Even though the depth of feelings felt after losing a pet can be overwhelming, we can start the healing process by accepting and recognizing these emotions. Remind yourself that it is acceptable to experience feelings of regret, guilt, or sadness. Seeking support from others as well as being able to rely on yourself are also crucial steps in the healing process. You can gradually find peace by acknowledging your feelings and taking solace in shared experiences.

As we continue our exploration of pet-loss grief, Chapter 3 will guide you through the various stages of sorrow and the unanticipated emotions that accompany this journey.

Chapter 3:

Riding the Emotional Rollercoaster

The loss of a beloved pet can feel like a sudden, gut-wrenching drop, a free fall of emotions that leaves you disoriented and breathless. But then, despite being a complex and intensely personal experience, it unfolds in its own time.

By understanding the stages during mourning and practicing self-care even when it's most difficult to do so, you can steer through this emotional storm and emerge stronger on the other side. This is why we will explore the ups and downs of grief that come with losing a cherished pet in this chapter.

Understanding the Stages of Grief

The experience of grief is intricate, very personal, and frequently develops in phases. Psychologist Elisabeth Kübler-Ross first described these stages in her seminal work, *On Death and Dying*. The five stages of grief, according to Kübler-Ross, are denial, anger, bargaining, depression, and acceptance (Kübler-Ross, n.d.). Although there is a framework for understanding the stages of grief, it isn't a linear process. You might go through the phases more than once or in a different order. Every stage presents unique obstacles and chances for development, culminating in acceptance and recovery. Let us take a closer look at each phase and discover how to get through grief's emotional maze.

The Stages of Grief: A Brief Overview

So far, we've come to understand that losing a beloved pet can set off a whirlwind of emotions that may feel overwhelming and all-encompassing. Knowing the phases of grief can help you get through this trying period. The five typical stages of grief, as defined by Elisabeth Kübler-Ross, are as follows:

Denial

This is frequently how people react to loss at first. As a buffer, denial helps to dull the pain and shock at first. You may find it difficult to accept that your pet has truly passed away at this point. Thoughts like *This can't be happening* or *Maybe it's a mistake* are common. Denial gives you time to progressively come to terms with reality while enabling you to endure the immediate aftermath of loss.

Anger

It is normal to feel angry as the reality of your loss starts to set in. You may be angry at the circumstance, other people, or even at yourself. You may be angry at yourself for things you believe you could have done differently or frustrated about the circumstances surrounding your pet's death. It is critical to realize that feeling angry is a normal and essential aspect of the healing process.

Bargaining

At this point, you may find yourself attempting, in vain, to undo the damage or lessen the hurt by striking deals or making promises. It is not uncommon to think thoughts like, *I would do anything to have them back* or *If only I had taken them to the vet sooner.* Bargaining is a way to regain a sense of control during a time that feels very out of control.

Depression

Deep sadness and a sense of emptiness are hallmarks of this stage. You may have a deep sense of loss, cry a lot, or feel cut off from your regular pursuits and hobbies. This is often the longest stage, and it can come and go in waves. It's important to allow yourself to feel this sadness and seek support if it becomes overwhelming.

Acceptance

To accept a loss is not to forget it or to "get over" it. Instead, it refers to coming to a place where you can accept the loss as real and figure out how to live with it. With acceptance, you can start to integrate your pet's memory into your life in a healthy way and remember them with more love than pain.

The Stages of Grief

These stages don't follow a neat, straightforward path. You might go through them in a different order or go through some of the stages more than once. Each stage's duration and intensity can also differ significantly between pet owners. There is no "correct" way to grieve; how you do so is unique to you. Having patience with yourself and letting things happen organically is important.

Knowing these phases can assist you in realizing that what you are going through is a typical reaction to loss. It is acceptable to experience the whole spectrum of feelings and to need some time to recover. We will go into more detail about each step in the sections that follow, providing you with coping mechanisms and insights to help you along the way.

Denial: The Initial Shock and Disbelief

First, when a beloved pet passes away, the initial shock can be so intense that your mind struggles to fully grasp the reality of their absence. This stage of denial can act as an emotional buffer, giving you time to adjust to the overwhelming loss. However, it can also hold you back from properly grieving. Denial can manifest as disbelief or numbness, making it difficult to start the healing process. It's important to recognize and understand this stage, as acknowledging the loss is the first step toward acceptance and healing.

Recognizing the Initial Stage of Denial

In the initial stage of denial, your mind might refuse to accept that your pet is truly gone. You may find yourself expecting to see them when you walk through the door or hear their familiar sounds around the house. This is your brain's way of trying to protect you from the immediate pain of the loss. Acknowledging these feelings as part of the denial stage can help you understand that it's a normal reaction and that it's okay to feel this way.

Denial can manifest in several ways:

- **Expecting to see your pet:** You might instinctively look for your pet in their usual spots or think you hear them moving around.

- **Routine habits:** You might catch yourself preparing their food or getting ready for a walk out of habit, only to be jolted back to reality when you realize they're no longer there.

- **Emotional numbness:** Feeling emotionally numb or detached can be a sign of denial, as it shields you from the immediate impact of the loss.

Breaking Through Denial With Gentle Strategies

While denial offers a reprieve, it's important to begin processing the loss. Here are some gentle strategies to help you navigate this stage:

- **Acknowledge your feelings.** Suppressing denial only prolongs it. Accept that denial is a natural part of grief and allow yourself to feel the disbelief or numbness.

- **Maintain a connection.** Surrounding yourself with mementos or photos of your pet can help keep their memory alive. Consider creating a memory box or a scrapbook filled with pictures and cherished keepsakes.

- **Talk about your pet.** Sharing stories and memories with loved ones who understand your bond with your pet can be cathartic. Talking about the good times and the loss can help you begin to process your emotions.

- **Seek support groups.** Connecting with others who have experienced pet loss can be incredibly helpful. Online forums or support groups can provide a safe space to share your feelings and learn from others' experiences.

- **Allow yourself to grieve.** There's no right or wrong way to grieve. Cry if you need to, scream into a pillow, or write down your feelings in a journal. Allowing yourself to express your grief is an essential part of moving on.

Remember, denial is a temporary stage, not a permanent state. By recognizing its signs, practicing self-compassion, and seeking support, you can gently move through and start to heal.

Moments of Denial Following Sophie and Simon's Deaths

After Sophie passed away, I remember the first few days were filled with a surreal sense of disbelief. Dropping her and Simon off at the groomer had been part of our routine, and hearing that Sophie had died felt like a bad dream. I kept expecting to see her wagging her tail when I walked through the door, and the silence was unbearable. Feeding time became a painful reminder of her absence. I'd prepare her food, only to realize she wasn't there to eat it.

When Simon passed away, it was another blow. He had adapted quickly to being the only dog, and our bond had deepened. Coming home to find him gone felt like losing Sophie all over again. I would instinctively call out his name, expecting to hear his bark or see him hiding under the bed. The routine of looking for him, only to find emptiness, was a harsh reminder that he was truly gone.

These moments of denial, when I struggled to accept their absence, were filled with intense emotional pain. The familiar routines that once brought joy now become painful memories. Each time I faced an empty food bowl or an untouched toy, it brought back the reality of their loss that much more. It truly was heartbreaking.

Even though it may seem challenging, it is important to identify and acknowledge these denial-based feelings. It is a step in the grieving process that enables you to accept the loss gradually. You can begin to move past denial and take the first steps toward healing by realizing that it is a normal reaction.

Anger: Dealing With Intense Emotions

After the initial shock and denial of losing a beloved pet, a storm of anger often brews within. This stage can be particularly tumultuous, fueled by a potent cocktail of emotions like injustice, frustration, and helplessness. Understanding that these feelings are a normal part of grieving is crucial. Recognizing and navigating this anger is a vital step toward healing, allowing you to process your emotions healthily.

Exploring the Rage Stage

Within grief lies the rage stage. Here, you might find yourself lashing out in unexpected ways, experiencing a range of emotions from mild annoyance to burning wrath. You might grapple with the unfairness of it all, questioning why your furry companion had to leave you.

- **Annoyance:** Seemingly trivial things can suddenly become major irritants. You might find yourself snapping at well-meaning friends who offer unsolicited advice or feeling frustrated by the constant reminders of your pet's absence.

- **Wrath:** Periods of intense anger might consume you, leaving you feeling overwhelmed by the depth of your loss. This anger can be directed outward, toward the world, the vet who couldn't save them, or even inward, at yourself for something you think you could have done differently.

- **Unfairness:** A sense of injustice can permeate this stage. You might find yourself asking existential questions like, *Why did this have to happen?* or *Why couldn't they have lived a longer life?* These questions, though unanswerable, are a natural part of processing the unfairness of losing a loved one.

Weathering the Storm by Processing and Expressing Anger

Finding healthy ways to process and express this anger is vital for your emotional well-being. Suppressing it can lead to prolonged grief and exacerbate stress. Here are some effective tools to work through your anger:

- **Journaling:** Pour your heart out onto paper. Journaling allows you to express your anger without judgment and gain insight into your grief. Write down the questions that plague you, the frustrations that consume you, and the memories that bring both joy and sorrow.

- **Physical activity:** Exercise is a fantastic way to release pent-up tension and anger. Activities like running, swimming, or even a brisk walk can help clear your head and provide a healthy outlet for your emotions. Consider engaging in activities that combine physical exertion with mental focus, such as martial arts.

- **Creative expression:** Art can be a powerful tool for healing. Painting, drawing, sculpting, or even playing a musical instrument can help you constructively express your anger.

Transform your pain into something tangible, a tribute to the love you shared with your pet.

- **Talking it out:** Sometimes, simply talking about your feelings can make a world of difference. Find a supportive and nonjudgmental listener, a friend, family member, or therapist who can offer a listening ear and validate your experience. Sharing your grief with someone who understands can lessen the feeling of isolation and help you move forward.

Remember, anger is a natural part of the grieving process. By acknowledging these emotions and finding healthy ways to express and process them, you can navigate this stage with courage and self-compassion. As you move through the stages of grief, each one, even the stormy ones, brings you closer to acceptance and healing.

Bargaining and Looking for Meaning and Solutions

This stage is a desperate search for meaning and a yearning to rewrite the past. Filled with a potent mix of sorrow and a flicker of hope, you might find yourself making deals with fate or a higher power, desperately seeking a way to alter the past or influence the future to bring your beloved companion back. Bargaining is a coping mechanism, a way to shield yourself from the overwhelming pain of loss by clinging to the possibility that things could have been different.

Navigating the Bargaining Table

The bargaining stage is often characterized by a fervent attempt to negotiate your way out of the crushing pain of loss. This might involve making promises to change specific behaviors, striking deals with fate itself, or pleading with a higher power for a different reality. It's a natural response to the helplessness that accompanies grief, offering a temporary sense of control in an otherwise uncontrollable situation.

- **Renegotiating the past:** You might find your mind replaying "what-if" scenarios, bargaining with fate through thoughts like, *If only I had taken them to the vet sooner* or *If only I had noticed the signs* *earlier, maybe things would be different.* These thoughts, fueled by a desire to understand and make sense of the loss, are a natural part of the grieving process.

- **Appealing to a higher power:** It's not uncommon to find solace in prayer or making deals with a higher power. You might find yourself promising to be a better person, to make significant life changes, or even devote yourself to a cause in exchange for your pet's return. This act of seeking solace and connection to something greater than yourself during a time of profound loss can be a source of comfort.

A Personal Story

My grief journey after losing Sophie and Simon was filled with countless moments of bargaining. I vividly remember nights spent wrestling with God, silently pleading for a different outcome.

Sophie's Farewell

In the aftermath of Sophie's unexpected passing, a wave of regret and a desperate need for answers washed over me. I couldn't escape the thought that *If only I hadn't been so tired that day and groomed them myself, maybe Sophie would still be here.* This bargaining manifested in promises to take better care of myself and my remaining pets, a desperate hope that, somehow, these actions could undo the tragedy. Every fiber of my being yearned to go back in time and change that fateful day.

Simon's Loss

When Simon succumbed to a pulmonary embolism, the shock and grief were almost unbearable. My mind replayed the events on a loop, searching for any missed signs and any action I could have taken differently. Thoughts like, *If only I had taken him for more frequent check-ups* or *If only I had noticed something was wrong sooner* echoed relentlessly. Silently bargaining, I vowed to be more vigilant and attentive in the future, hoping somehow it could bring Simon back.

These moments of bargaining, though intensely painful, were a crucial part of my healing process. They allowed me to confront my feelings of guilt and helplessness and to slowly begin accepting the reality of my pets' deaths. Bargaining can be a way to process grief and eventually move toward acceptance, even if it means facing uncomfortable truths and letting go of the "what-ifs."

As you move forward and understand that bargaining is a natural response to grief, you can navigate this challenging stage with self-compassion.

Depression: Exploring the Depths of Grief

After the initial shock, anger, and bargaining have subsided, the true weight of your loss settles in, ushering in the stage of depression. This stage is a dark valley shrouded in tremendous sadness, a sense of emptiness so vast that it seems to swallow you whole. Hopelessness becomes a constant companion, painting the future with a bleak, colorless brushstroke. While undeniably challenging, understand that depression is a natural part of the grieving process, a necessary descent into the depths of your sorrow.

Recognizing Depression's Many Faces

Depression and grief can manifest in a multitude of ways, each a reflection of the immense loss you've experienced.

- **Crippling sadness:** You might find yourself drowning in a sea of tears, the well of sorrow seemingly bottomless. A deep, persistent ache settles in your chest, a constant reminder of the absence you now endure. This sadness is evidence of the love you shared with your pet, a reflection of the significant void their passing has left.

- **Loss of interest:** Activities that once brought vibrant colors to your life now appear dull and meaningless. Social gatherings, hobbies you cherished, and routines that provided comfort all lose their appeal. The world around you seems muted, a reflection of the emptiness within.

- **The grip of hopelessness:** A suffocating sense of hopelessness can take hold, leaving you convinced the sadness will never lift. The future stretches out before you, a desolate wasteland devoid of joy or purpose. This feeling may be accompanied by a numbing indifference, a lack of motivation to engage with the world, or even care for yourself.

Recognizing these feelings as a natural response to your loss is crucial. Depression, though undeniably difficult, signifies that you're actively processing your grief, confronting the raw and painful emotions that accompany it.

Strategies for Coping With Depression

Coping with this stage of grief is essential for your emotional and mental well-being. Here are some strategies you can use to help you with your sorrow:

- **Seeking professional help:** Don't hesitate to reach out for professional support. A therapist or counselor specializing in pet loss can provide invaluable tools and guidance to help you through this difficult time. Therapy offers a safe space to express your feelings, explore your grief, and develop healthy coping mechanisms.

- **Prioritizing self-care:** Taking care of your physical and mental health is paramount during this time. Engage in activities that nourish your body and soul, such as regular exercise, healthy eating, and ensuring you get enough sleep. Creative outlets like writing, painting, or playing music can also be incredibly therapeutic, allowing you to express your emotions in a cathartic way.

- **Finding strength in numbers:** Connecting with a pet-loss support group can provide much-needed comfort and understanding. Sharing your experiences with others who have walked a similar path can alleviate the feeling of isolation and remind you that you're not alone.

The reason why this is important to do is because, by acknowledging your feelings and actively seeking healthy coping mechanisms, you can begin to manage the depression stage of grief. Remember, be patient with yourself. Allow yourself the time and space to grieve. Though the path ahead may seem long and arduous, know that there is a light at the end of this tunnel.

Embracing the Reality of Loss

Acceptance, the final stage of grief, is not about forgetting your beloved pet or pretending the pain never existed. It's about acknowledging the harsh reality of their absence while finding a way to carry their memory forward and embrace life anew. Acceptance is a slow, gradual process, a gentle shift from the raw ache of loss to a place of peaceful remembrance. Yes, the pain is unbearable, but even as difficult as it may sound, reaching acceptance doesn't happen overnight. It's a journey paved with moments of reflection and a dawning realization that your furry friend is no longer physically present. The sharp sting of grief softens, replaced by a bittersweet fondness. You'll find yourself reminiscing about shared adventures and playful moments, and then eventually a smile replaces the tears.

Acceptance doesn't erase the sadness or wipe away the memories. It signifies you've found a way to coexist with the loss. You've integrated the memory of your pet into your life, a source of comfort rather than constant sorrow. The intense grief will eventually transform into a gentler, more reflective state of remembrance.

Finding Ways to Cope and Move Forward

Always remember that acceptance isn't about erasing the past but about building a new relationship with it. Here are some ways to find solace and begin moving forward:

- **Creating a tribute:** Many find comfort in creating a memorial for their pet. This could be a dedicated space in your home, a lovingly curated scrapbook filled with photos and stories, or a piece of jewelry that reminds you of their presence.

- **Rituals of remembrance:** Rituals offer a sense of closure and honor your pet's memory. Lighting a candle on their birthday, visiting a favorite park you shared, or participating in a pet remembrance ceremony are all ways to keep their spirit alive.

- **Carrying on their legacy:** Finding ways to continue your pet's legacy can be incredibly healing. Volunteering at an animal shelter, donating to a cause you champion, or even welcoming another pet into your life when you're ready are all ways to keep their spirit alive.

- **Keeping the conversation alive:** Talk about your pet with loved ones. Sharing stories and memories not only keeps their memory vibrant but also allows you to express your grief in a supportive environment.

Acceptance is a delicate balance between cherishing the past and embracing the future. It's a sign that you're starting to heal, not a sign of forgetting. While moments of sadness may still arise, they will lessen in frequency and intensity. By embracing acceptance, you can continue to honor the love and joy your pet brought into your life, all while creating a path toward a fulfilling future.

Recognizing How Your Grief Has Manifested

Grief is a deeply personal experience, developed by facets of your unique personality, past experiences, and the close bond you shared with your pet. Understanding how grief manifests in you can be a powerful tool for navigating this emotional terrain with greater self-awareness and compassion.

Exploring Grief

Grief expresses itself in a multitude of ways, as unique as the pet owners experiencing it. Some may find themselves awash in a sea of emotions, their sorrow a visible storm. Others may appear stoic on the surface, their grief a quieter undercurrent. You might even experience a bit of both. The circumstances surrounding your pet's passing, the depth of your connection, and your inherent coping mechanisms all influence how grief manifests within you.

Embracing Your Path Through the Valley of Tears

Remember, there's no single path mandated by grief. Each person's journey is as distinctive as their fingerprint, shaped by their experiences, beliefs, and the ever-shifting emotional landscape. Comparing your grief with another's or feeling pressured to conform to societal expectations can only add to the weight you carry. Instead, embrace your unique mourning process with acceptance and self-compassion.

Finding Solace on the Path With Techniques and Patterns

As you walk the path of grief, you might find solace in various coping mechanisms and grief patterns. Some might seek solace in quiet reflection, allowing themselves the space to process their emotions in solitude. Others may find comfort in the embrace of loved ones, drawing strength from shared memories and understanding.

No matter what specific coping mechanisms you discover, the key lies in finding what works best for you and honoring your needs and feelings every step of the way. Your experience with grief is deeply personal, and by approaching it with openness and self-kindness, you can move toward healing and acceptance at your own pace and in your way.

Weathering the Storm of Intense Emotions

Steps Toward Healing

Yes, it's true that the intense waves of sadness and loneliness following the loss of a pet can feel overwhelming, and this is perfectly normal. However, there are strategies to help you manage these emotions and find pockets of solace along the way.

Step 1: Permission to Feel

One of the most crucial steps in coping with intense emotions is allowing yourself to fully experience them. Don't suppress or deny your feelings. Give yourself permission to acknowledge and express them in healthy ways. Whether it's pouring your heart out in a journal, expressing your emotions through art, or simply talking to a trusted friend, finding creative outlets for your grief can provide a much-needed release and a sense of relief.

Step 2: Channeling Emotions Into Art

Grief, though a heavy weight to carry, can be transformed through the power of creativity. Engaging in creative activities can be a powerful tool for healing, allowing you to express the complex emotions swirling within you in a safe and cathartic way. Whether you find solace in writing heartfelt poems, capturing memories on canvas, or pouring your emotions into music, creative expression offers a unique outlet for your grief.

By expressing your feelings through creative endeavors, you not only honor the memory of your beloved pet but also begin the process of healing. The act of creation can be incredibly therapeutic, allowing you to process your emotions tangibly. For example, a poem penned with love can become a testament to the unique bond you shared. A painting splashed with vibrant colors can capture the joy your pet brought into your life. A melody composed with raw emotion can express the depth of your loss.

Step 3: Reaching Out for a Connection

The loss of a pet can leave a gaping hole in your life, a deep loneliness that daily routines and companionship once filled. It's important to acknowledge these feelings rather than suppress them. Reach out to supportive friends and family members who can offer a listening ear and a comforting embrace. Don't hesitate to seek out pet-loss support groups, either online or in person. Connecting with others who have walked a similar path can alleviate the feeling of isolation and provide a sense of shared understanding. You'll find strength in their stories and comfort in knowing you're not alone in your grief.

Step 4: Finding Solace in Routine and Establishing New Rituals

While the absence of your pet may disrupt your established routines, creating new rituals and habits can provide a much-needed sense of stability and comfort. Consider incorporating daily walks in nature, a practice that can be both physically and mentally grounding. Mindfulness meditation can offer a space for quiet reflection and emotional processing. Even creating a cozy corner in your home—a space dedicated to remembering your pet and unwinding—can become a source of solace.

Step 5: Prioritizing Self-Care and Building Resilience

As you navigate the waves of grief, remember to prioritize self-care above all else. Allow yourself ample time to rest and recharge. Nourish your body with healthy foods and prioritize activities that bring you joy and relaxation. Taking care of your physical and emotional well-being is essential for building resilience and building the strength you need to cope with the intense emotions that accompany pet loss. By embracing creative expression, reaching out for connection, establishing comforting routines, and prioritizing self-care, you can begin to heal, carrying the cherished memories of your furry companion close to your heart.

Healthy Strategies for Rage

Losing your pet can ignite a firestorm of anger within you. It's perfectly normal to feel enraged—at God, at the circumstances, or even at yourself. The key is to find healthy outlets to express and process these intense emotions before they consume you.

Here are some effective coping strategies to help you manage your rage constructively:

Channeling Fury Through Movement and Physical Activity

Physical activity is a fantastic way to release pent-up anger and tension. Whether it's a brisk walk in nature or hitting the gym for a vigorous workout, exercise helps channel your energy into productive outlets. As you move your body, endorphins kick in, promoting feelings of relaxation and well-being, and creating a natural antidote to anger.

Taking Action

1. Find something you genuinely like, be it dancing, swimming, or team sports. This increases the likelihood that you'll stick with it.

2. Block out a dedicated time each day to move your body. Remember, consistency is key.

3. While exercising, concentrate on the sensations of movement and the rhythm of your breath. Be fully present and in the moment.

4. Immerse yourself completely in the activity. As your body moves, allow negative emotions to flow out with each step, breath, or swing.

Expressing Anger on Paper

Writing a letter to your pet can be a therapeutic way to process your anger and gain clarity on your feelings. Pour your frustrations, grievances, and regrets onto the page. This act of expression can provide a sense of release and closure. It allows you to articulate and confront your emotions in a safe space, away from the potential for outbursts.

Taking Action

1. Seek a comfortable, distraction-free environment where you can write freely.

2. Begin the letter by speaking directly to your beloved companion.

3. Write openly and freely about your anger, holding nothing back. Be as honest and expressive as possible.

4. After writing, take a moment to reread your letter. Consider any insights or resolutions that might emerge from this process.

Finding Calm in the Storm With Mindfulness Activities

Mindfulness practices can help you cultivate awareness of your anger and develop healthier ways of responding to it. Techniques like deep breathing and meditation can help you observe and acknowledge your emotions without judgment. This allows you to respond with greater clarity and compassion.

Taking Action

1. Find a quiet, comfortable place where you can sit or lie down comfortably.

2. Close your eyes and take several deep breaths, focusing on the sensation of air entering and leaving your body.

3. Bring your attention to the physical sensations of anger in your body, such as tightness in your chest or tension in your muscles.

4. Allow yourself to fully experience these sensations without trying to change them.

5. As you continue to breathe deeply, imagine sending waves of compassion and understanding to yourself, soothing the anger and promoting inner peace.

Understanding and Processing Anger After Pet Loss

The sudden absence of a cherished pet can leave you grappling with a whirlwind of emotions, and anger is a perfectly natural one. It's important to acknowledge this anger and process it in healthy ways rather than bottling it up. By recognizing and validating your anger, you can begin to understand its roots and make your way toward healing and resolution.

Validating Your Anger

Anger is a natural response to loss. It arises from the pain of losing your furry companion, the frustration of a situation you couldn't control, or even anger directed at yourself. Suppressing or denying these emotions can hinder the healing process. Allow yourself to acknowledge your anger and accept it as a valid part of your grief. Remember, anger is a signal that something needs attention. By listening to this signal with compassion, you can address the underlying causes of your pain and find inner peace.

Prioritizing Self-Care

Self-care is an essential pillar during the grieving process. Grief can be emotionally and physically draining, so taking care of yourself is crucial for building resilience and fostering the strength you need to cope. Here are some practical self-care strategies to support your well-being:

- Ensure you're getting enough sleep each night. Establishing a relaxing bedtime routine and creating a sleep-conducive environment are key.

- Prioritize healthy, balanced meals rich in essential nutrients. Focus on fruits, vegetables, whole grains, and lean proteins to support your physical and emotional well-being.

- Dedicate time to activities that bring you joy and comfort. Whether it's painting, reading, listening to music, or spending time in nature, these hobbies offer a welcome distraction and promote relaxation.

Finding Solace and Joy With Moments of Light in the Darkness

Grief doesn't have to consume you entirely—you need to find moments of solace and joy to nurture your spirit and uplift your mood. These moments of connection and rejuvenation can help you rediscover hope in the face of sadness.

Take leisurely walks in nature, pursue creative endeavors, or spend quality time with loved ones. These simple acts can bring comfort and remind you that joy still exists.

Prioritizing self-care and finding moments of joy are not indulgences, but essential tools for navigating grief with greater ease. By tending to your physical and emotional needs, you cultivate inner strength and resilience. This allows you to cope with the challenges of pet loss while cherishing the memory of your beloved companion. Remember, self-care is not selfish but an act of self-compassion during a difficult time.

*****

In this chapter, we've explored the various stages and manifestations of grief that accompany the loss of a beloved pet. From denial to acceptance, each stage presents its unique challenges and opportunities for healing. By understanding and acknowledging the complexity of our emotions, we can navigate the ups and downs of the grieving process with greater clarity and compassion.

Through self-care practices and coping strategies, we can prioritize our well-being and find moments of solace and joy amid the sadness. Remember that grief is a personal experience, and it's okay to seek support and guidance as you ride the rollercoaster of emotions.

As we continue our exploration of pet-loss grief, let's challenge social stigmas and embrace the uniqueness of our grief experiences. In Chapter 4, join me as we explore the importance of honoring our individual grief and resisting societal pressures to conform to rigid expectations of mourning.

Chapter 4:

How I grieve Is Personal

Though society frequently downplays the intensity of this grief, losing a pet is a very personal and emotional experience.

In this chapter, we will address the myths and taboos surrounding pet loss, encouraging you to embrace your emotions and honor your unique grieving process. We'll explore the societal pressures that can complicate mourning and discuss ways to challenge and overcome these stigmas, allowing you to grieve authentically and without shame.

As I've mentioned before, grief is not a one-size-fits-all experience, and the loss of a pet can evoke a wide range of emotions that deserve recognition and respect. By confronting the social stigmas that minimize pet loss, we can create a more compassionate and understanding environment for ourselves and others who are mourning the loss of a beloved animal companion.

Addressing Myths About Pet-Loss Grief

When it comes to grieving the loss of a pet, many people encounter societal myths and misconceptions that can make the process even more challenging. Understanding and dispelling these myths is very important because it allows us to validate our emotions and mourn our pets healthily and authentically. By recognizing the reality of our grief, we can better understand the healing process and honor the bond we shared with our beloved animal companions.

Busting Common Myths

Myth 1: "It's just a pet; get over it."

One of the most pervasive myths about pet loss is the idea that because a pet is not human, the grief we feel should be minimal and short-lived. This dismissive attitude ignores the immense emotional connections that many of us form with our pets. Pets are integral parts of our lives, offering unconditional love, companionship, and joy. Grieving their loss is natural and valid, and it's important to allow ourselves the time and space to process this grief fully.

Myth 2: "You can always get another one."

While it's true that we can welcome new pets into our lives, this statement overlooks the unique and irreplaceable bond we had with the pets we lost. Each pet has its own personality, quirks, and history with us, making the relationship special and unique. Suggesting that a new pet can simply replace the lost one diminishes the significance of our bond and the depth of our sorrow. It's essential to recognize that while new pets can bring joy and companionship, they do not erase the love and memories we share with our departed pets.

Myth 3: "Grief over a pet isn't as valid as grief over a human loved one."

This myth stems from the societal hierarchy that often places human relationships above all else. However, the emotional impact of losing a pet can be just as profound as losing a human loved one. Pets are often our confidants, companions, and sources of emotional support. Their loss can leave a significant void in our lives; our grief is no less real or valid because it's for an animal.

Myth 4: "Crying over a pet is a sign of weakness."

Some people may believe that expressing deep sorrow over a pet's death is a sign of emotional weakness or immaturity. In reality, showing our emotions is a sign of strength and emotional intelligence. It takes courage to face our grief head-on and to express our feelings openly. Crying and mourning are natural parts of the healing process and should be embraced rather than suppressed.

Myth 5: "You should be over it by now."

Grief has no set timeline, and everyone processes loss differently. Some people may find solace and acceptance relatively quickly, while others may struggle with their grief for a longer period of time. There is no right or wrong way to grieve, and it's important to be patient with ourselves and others as we get through our pet loss.

Myth 6: "Talking about your pet all the time means you're not moving on."

Sharing memories and stories about our lost pets can be a vital part of the healing process. It helps keep their memory alive and allows us to process our grief. Talking about our pets does not mean we are stuck in the past; rather, it can be a way of integrating the love and lessons they brought into our present lives.

Myth 7: "Having a funeral or a memorial for a pet is over the top."

Honoring a pet with a funeral, a memorial, or another ritual can be an important part of the grieving process. These acts of remembrance provide a sense of closure and allow us to celebrate the life of our pet. Such rituals can be deeply healing and should be respected as meaningful expressions of our love and loss.

These statements by others have made many doubt their grief and end up with conflicting emotions; however, by addressing and dispelling these myths, we can create a more compassionate understanding of pet loss and grief. It's essential to acknowledge that our feelings are valid and that mourning the loss of a pet is a deeply personal and significant experience. Embracing this understanding helps us and others learn to manage the complex emotions that come with saying goodbye to our cherished animal companions.

Accurate Facts and Studies to Demonstrate the Importance of Grieving

When we experience the loss of a pet, the intensity of our grief can be overwhelming and often misunderstood by those around us. However, numerous studies and factual accounts highlight the importance of acknowledging and processing this grief, demonstrating that it's a significant and valid emotional experience. Here are some key points supported by research that underline the importance of pet loss grieving:

The Human-Animal Bond

Research has consistently shown that the bond between humans and their pets can be as strong as the bond between humans. According to the American Veterinary Medical Association (AVMA), pets can play a very important role in our emotional well-being, often acting as companions, confidants, and sources of unconditional love (*Human-animal bond | American Veterinary Medical Association*, n.d.). This deep connection explains why the loss of a pet can be as devastating as the loss of a human loved one.

The Psychological Impact of Pet Loss

Studies have found that the grief experienced after the loss of a pet can mirror that of losing a close family member. A study published in 2019 revealed that pet owners often experience significant levels of grief, including symptoms such as depression, anxiety, and loneliness after their pet dies (Uccheddu et al., 2019). This underscores the need for society to recognize and support those mourning the loss of their pets.

The Therapeutic Benefits of Mourning

Acknowledging and processing grief is an essential part of healing. Grieving enables people to accept their loss and start the process of emotional healing. Psychologists stress that ignoring or repressing grief can result in complicated grief or even protracted suffering, which can seriously hinder a person's capacity to go about their daily lives. We can process our feelings and come up with coping mechanisms for our loss when we permit ourselves to grieve (Mughal & Siddiqui, 2019).

The Role of Social Support

The grieving process is greatly aided by social support. A study published in *The Veterinary Journal* emphasized how important it is for people who are mourning the loss of a pet to have networks of support. Friends, family members, support groups, and even vets can provide empathy, understanding, and validation, which are essential for healing (Pilgram, 2010). Sharing memories and talking about the pet with others who understand can help alleviate feelings of isolation and loneliness.

The Positive Impact of Memorializing Pets

Creating rituals or memorials for pets can be a therapeutic way to honor their memory and find closure. Studies suggest that participating in these kinds of activities can assist people in coping with their loss and preserving their relationship with their pets. Memorials offer a material means of honoring the pet's life and legacy, such as planting a tree, making a photo album, or hosting a small ceremony (Packman et al., 2012).

The Healing Power of Acknowledgement

Acknowledging the significance of pet-loss grief can lead to better mental health outcomes. When pet loss is recognized and validated by society, individuals are more likely to seek help and support, which can facilitate the healing process. Mental health professionals advocate for the normalization of pet-loss grief and encourage individuals to seek counseling or support groups if needed (Chakma et al., 2021).

Case Studies on Pet-Loss Grief

Several case studies have highlighted the profound impact of pet loss on individuals' lives. Many people experienced severe depression following the death of their pets. Through therapy that acknowledged the importance of their grief and helped them process their emotions, they were able to find a path toward healing. This shows the need for empathetic and informed approaches to pet-loss grief (*My experience of losing a pet and what helped my recovery*, n.d.).

These facts and studies show one thing: We can better appreciate the importance of grieving our pets by accepting and acknowledging that, without it, the pain from the loss puts a mental and emotional burden on pet owners. This knowledge helps validate our feelings and encourages us to seek the support and resources needed to work through these challenging emotions.

It's a fact that grieving the loss of a pet is not just a sign of love and connection; it's also a very important step toward healing and honoring the cherished memories of our beloved companions.

Validity of Grief

The Enormous Impact That Pets Have on Our Lives

Pets hold an incredibly significant place in our lives, often becoming more than just animals we care for—they become family. From the moment we bring them into our homes, they start to shape our daily routines, influence our emotional well-being, and create lasting memories. The joy of a wagging tail when you return home, the comfort of a warm purr on your lap, and the unconditional love they offer all contribute to a bond that is deeply enriching. This relationship is filled with shared experiences and mutual trust, and it often fills a void that nothing else can. The impact of this connection is so profound that losing a pet can leave a significant emotional void, making the grief experienced both intense and entirely valid.

The grief that accompanies the death of a pet can be as deep and as painful as the loss of a human loved one—the relationship we share with our pets is often one of pure, unconditional love and companionship. Pets are there for us during our best and worst times, providing comfort without judgment and companionship without expectations. They are a constant presence in our lives, and their absence can be profoundly felt. The routines that were built around their care and the moments of joy they brought are stark reminders of their loss. This depth of grief is not only understandable but also deserving of recognition and respect.

The Genuine Bond Between a Pet and Its Owner

The bond between a pet and its owner is a genuine, loving relationship that deserves to be mourned when lost. Unlike many human relationships, the connection with a pet is often uncomplicated by misunderstandings or conflicts. It's a pure relationship built on a foundation of loyalty, trust, and unconditional love. Pets do not hold grudges, and they do not criticize—they simply offer a love that is unwavering and steadfast. This unique bond means that when a pet passes away, the sense of loss can be all-encompassing.

Mourning the loss of a pet is a natural and necessary process. It acknowledges the value and significance of the relationship and allows for the expression of love and sorrow. Just as with human relationships, the process of grieving a pet helps in processing the loss and beginning to heal. It's important to recognize that the emotions felt during this time—whether they are sadness, anger, guilt, or loneliness—are valid. Society often minimizes pet-loss grief, but understanding and accepting it as a legitimate form of grief is very important for emotional well-being. In doing so, we honor the deep, loving connection we shared with our pets and permit ourselves to grieve in a healthy and meaningful way.

Cultural Approaches and Perspectives on Pet Loss

Grieving the loss of a pet can vary widely across different cultures and communities. These cultural differences can influence how individuals cope with the death of a pet and how society at large perceives and supports pet-loss grief. When it comes to abolishing myths, understanding these varied perspectives can help us appreciate the universal nature of this type of grief and provide insights into different ways to honor our beloved pets.

Cultural Differences in Grieving Practices

United States and Western Countries

In the US and many Western countries, pets are often considered part of the family. The grieving process for a pet can be very similar to that of a human family member. It's common for people to hold funerals or memorial services for their pets. Pet cemeteries and cremation services are available, and some people keep ashes in urns or create keepsakes such as paw-print molds and photo albums.

The societal acceptance of pet-loss grief in these cultures has grown, with many mental health professionals recognizing and supporting individuals through this type of grief. There are also support groups and online communities where people can share their experiences and find solace.

Japan

In Japan, pets are often seen as spiritual beings that deserve respect and proper rituals upon their death. Pet funerals are quite common, with many pet owners choosing to hold elaborate ceremonies similar to those for humans. Some temples offer services specifically for pets, including memorial rites and prayer offerings.

The concept of a pet being a member of the family is strong, and there are various memorial products and services available, such as personalized gravestones and Buddhist ceremonies, to ensure the pet's peaceful transition to the afterlife. This cultural approach shows the deep respect and emotional attachment Japanese people often feel toward their pets.

Mexico

In Mexican culture, the Day of the Dead, or *Día de los Muertos*, is a significant tradition where families honor deceased loved ones, including pets. It's believed that the spirits of the deceased return to visit their living relatives during this time, and altars, or *ofrendas*, are set up with offerings of food, photographs, and other memorabilia.

Pets are often included in these altars, with their pictures and favorite treats placed alongside those of human family members. This cultural practice highlights the belief in the enduring bond between the living and the deceased, recognizing pets as integral parts of the family who are remembered and celebrated.

With this knowledge about cultural differences and traditions, we can gain a deeper appreciation for the universal experience of pet loss and grief and recognize the importance of honoring and remembering our pets in meaningful ways.

Breaking the Silence by Encouraging Open Conversations

It's a sad notion, but in many places, pet loss and grief can be a taboo topic, especially in societies where pets are not universally regarded as family members. The reluctance to openly discuss the emotional impact of losing a pet can lead to feelings of isolation and invalidation for those experiencing this type of grief. Breaking the silence and encouraging open conversations about pet loss is very important in dismantling these stigmas and creating a supportive environment for healing. Let's look into this in more detail now.

Addressing the Taboo Aspect of Pet-Loss Grieving

In many cultures, there is a pervasive notion that grieving the loss of a pet is less significant or valid than grieving the loss of a human loved one. This misconception can make pet owners hesitant to express their sadness, fearing judgment or misunderstanding from others. After all, there are more than just a handful of us who care about the opinions of others as we try to satisfy societal norms. The result of this is often a suppression of genuine emotions, which can hinder the grieving process and lead to prolonged suffering.

The taboo around pet-loss grief can be attributed to several factors:

- **Cultural norms:** In societies where pets are not commonly considered part of the family, expressing deep sorrow over a pet's death may be seen as excessive or inappropriate.

- **Lack of awareness:** Many people may not understand the unbreakable bond between humans and their pets, leading them to underestimate the emotional impact of a pet's death.

- **Fear of judgment:** Those grieving a pet may fear that others will judge them for their intense feelings, leading to a reluctance to share their experiences.

We need to encourage open conversations about pet loss and grief to break down these stigmas. Sharing personal stories and emotions can help validate the experience of others and create a sense of community and understanding. It may not be the easiest thing to do, especially if you are a part of a society that does not acknowledge pet-loss grief. However, this doesn't mean that you shouldn't at least try. By opening up, you are not only acknowledging your grief, but you can also help others do the same.

Here are some ways to start these conversations and support one another:

- **Share your story.** Opening up about your experiences with pet loss can encourage others to do the same. This can be done through social media, support groups, or casual conversations with friends and family.

- **Listen with empathy.** When someone shares their grief over a pet, listen without judgment. Acknowledge their feelings and offer your support.

- **Create safe spaces.** Support groups, both online and in-person, can provide a safe environment for people to share their experiences and find solace in knowing they are not alone.

- **Educate others.** Raising awareness about the emotional impact of pet loss can help dispel myths and misconceptions. Share personal anecdotes that highlight the significance of the human–pet bond.

If we encourage open conversations about pet loss and grief, we can break down the barriers that prevent people from fully expressing their emotions. Sharing our stories and supporting one another can lead to a greater understanding and acceptance of this type of grief, ultimately creating a more compassionate and inclusive society. In other words, we, as pet owners who have experienced the loss of our furry loved ones, need to advocate for change.

The How of Advocating for Change

Imagine people experiencing the loss of their loved ones like a mother losing a daughter or a son losing his father. Now picture this loss as something that is expected to mean nothing. What would happen to people if they weren't allowed to grieve their family members or loved ones after their passing? What would happen to those people if society expected them to carry on with day-to-day tasks as though nothing had happened?

The same goes for a person who loses a pet. These furry beings aren't unimportant animals that we don't care about. They, too, are alive and share their time and love with us. We share good and bad times with them, which is why we refer to them as *pets*—there is more to who or what they are. They share important bonds with us, their owners. Like that little girl down the street who goes to the park every day to play with her fluffy dog. Or that old lady up the street who always has her pet cat on her lap. The naughty boy I see in the pet store all the time, getting food for his little fish back home. If these people had to lose their companions, should we really expect them to do nothing and then carry on as though their lives hadn't changed in any way? No, of course not. After all, we are human beings, and what sets us apart from any other creature is our emotions, our love for others, and our ability to care for living things that do not share our DNA. For this reason, it's important that we teach people that pet-loss grief is a real thing, and it must be acknowledged. To advocate, you can try a few of the following:

Establishing Safe Spaces for Grief

Creating safe spaces where people can express their grief openly and receive support is very important for those mourning the loss of a pet. These spaces provide a sense of community and validation, helping people navigate their emotions without fear of judgment or misunderstanding.

Pet-Loss Support Groups and Resources in Communities

One of the most effective ways to support those grieving the loss of a pet is by advocating for the establishment of pet-loss support groups within communities. These groups can serve as safe havens where pet owners can share their experiences, find comfort in the shared understanding of others, and receive guidance from facilitators trained in grief counseling. These include the following:

- **Local community centers:** Encourage local community centers to host regular pet-loss support group meetings. These meetings can provide a structured environment for pet owners to express their grief and receive support.

- **Veterinary clinics and animal shelters:** Advocate for veterinary clinics and animal shelters to offer or promote pet-loss support services. These establishments often serve as the first point of contact for grieving pet owners and can play a very important role in directing them to appropriate resources.

- **Online platforms:** Promote the creation and participation in online support groups and forums dedicated to pet-loss grief. Online platforms can reach a wider audience and provide support for those who might not have access to local groups.

Support Networks and Options

There are already several established resources and support networks available for those dealing with pet-loss grief, as we've seen before. By making this information readily accessible, you can help pet owners find the support they need during their time of mourning:

- **The Association for Pet Loss and Bereavement (APLB):** APLB offers various resources, including online support groups, counseling services, and educational materials to help individuals cope with the loss of a pet.

- **The Pet Loss Support Page:** This online resource provides a comprehensive list of hotlines, support groups, and counselors specializing in pet-loss grief.

- **Local hotlines and counseling services:** Many communities offer hotlines and counseling services specifically for pet loss. Providing information about these services through community bulletin boards, social media, and local veterinary clinics can help pet owners access the support they need.

By advocating for the creation of dedicated pet-loss support groups and making information about existing resources more accessible, we can help create an environment where pet owners feel safe to grieve and receive the support they need. This advocacy not only benefits those currently mourning the loss of a pet but also helps to shift societal perceptions of pet-loss grief, building greater understanding and compassion.

Promoting Awareness and Advocacy

Promoting awareness about the significance of grieving pets is essential for creating a more compassionate and understanding society. This can be achieved through various channels, including social media campaigns, public talks, and partnerships with animal welfare organizations. By sharing stories and facts about the emotional impact of losing a pet, we can help dispel misconceptions and encourage a more empathetic approach to those experiencing this type of grief. Following are a few ways to accomplish that:

- **Social media campaigns:** Utilize platforms like Facebook, Instagram, and X (Twitter) to share personal stories, infographics, and articles about pet-loss grief.

- **Public talks and workshops:** Organize events in community centers, schools, and workplaces to educate people about the emotional toll of pet loss and how they can support grieving pet owners.

- **Partnerships:** Collaborate with animal welfare organizations and veterinary clinics to spread awareness and provide resources for those in need.

Champions for Change

As someone who has experienced the deep sorrow of losing a pet, your voice and story are powerful. By sharing your experiences and advocating for greater recognition of pet-loss grief, you can help transform societal attitudes and support others going through similar pain. Becoming a champion for change means speaking up, educating others, and creating an environment where all forms of grief are acknowledged and respected. Let's go into this in more detail.

Educate Others: Friends, Family, and Colleagues

Helping those around you understand the impact of pet loss can make a significant difference. Here are some strategies you could use to educate others:

- **Share personal experiences.** Talk openly about your feelings and experiences with pet loss to help others empathize and understand.

- **Provide educational resources.** Share articles, books, and videos that explain the emotional depth of pet-loss grief and its similarities to other types of grief.

- **Encourage open conversations.** Create a safe space for discussions about pet loss by initiating conversations and encouraging others to share their thoughts and feelings.

Tools and Information to Help People Understand Pet-Loss Grief

Providing the right tools and information can help those around you better understand the significance of pet-loss grief. Here are some resources you could try:

- **Books:** I recommend the books *Goodbye, Friend: Healing Wisdom for Anyone Who Has Ever Lost a Pet* by Gary Kowalski or *The Pet Loss Companion* by Ken Dolan-Del Vecchio. *After the Rainbow Bridge* can also help you understand pet loss and grief, giving you the tools and information you need to slowly take yourself out of the uncertainty and move forward n the grieving process.

- **Websites:** Share links to websites like the Association for Pet Loss and Bereavement (APLB) and the Pet Loss Support Page, which offer extensive resources and support.

- **Support groups:** Inform others about local and online support groups where they can connect with people who have experienced similar losses.

By promoting awareness, advocating for change, and educating others, we can help create a society where pet-loss grief is acknowledged and supported, allowing those who mourn to find the compassion and understanding they need.

*****

In this chapter, we've challenged societal stigmas surrounding pet-loss grief and encouraged open conversations about this often-misunderstood form of mourning. By dispelling myths, discussing cultural perspectives, and advocating for change, we've taken steps toward creating a more supportive and compassionate environment for those grieving the loss of a beloved pet. Remember, your grief is valid, and you are not alone.

As we get ready to move into Chapter 5, we'll explore the immense impact our animal companions have on our lives and the enduring legacy they leave behind. Through reflection and introspection, we'll uncover the deeper significance of our relationships with our pets and discover how their presence continues to shape our lives, even after they're gone. Let's turn the next page to discover understanding, healing, and finding meaning during loss.

Chapter 5:

The Meaning of Pet Loss

In this chapter, we peel back the many layers of feelings and experiences that come with losing a beloved animal friend. We aim to highlight the enormous importance of these relationships in our lives as we explore the psychological ramifications of pet loss and work through the difficulties of the grieving process. Come along as we discover the lasting legacy of our cherished pets, journey into the depths of grief, and find comfort in our common experiences.

The Psychological Effects of Pet Loss

Research has shown that the emotional toll of losing a pet can be comparable to that of losing a human loved one. The relationship that develops between people and their animal companions goes beyond simple companionship; rather, it is a deep bond that greatly affects our mental health (Laderer, 2019).

It is clear that there are extensive and varied psychological ramifications to losing a pet as we make our way through the maze of grief. Gaining an understanding of these results is crucial for confirming the feelings of bereaved pet owners and raising awareness of the significant influence these relationships have on our mental health.

Grieving Journey From a Psychological Perspective

Psychological frameworks provide vital insights into the complex process of mourning, which is invaluable in our quest to understand the grieving process. The well-known Kübler-Ross model, which is frequently used to analyze human loss, and which we covered in Chapter 3, sheds light on the complex web of feelings that arise after a pet dies.

The five phases of mourning, while originally conceptualized in the context of human death, resonate deeply with pet owners grappling with the absence of their cherished companions.

We have gone over these stages a little, but just to recap, denial is the initial shock and disbelief that shroud our consciousness as we struggle to accept the reality of our pet's departure. Denial serves as a protective barrier, shielding us from the full weight of our emotions as we grapple with the profound sense of loss.

Anger is the intense feelings of frustration, resentment, and injustice that may surge to the forefront as we confront the unfairness of our pet's untimely demise. Anger becomes a coping mechanism—a raw expression of the pain and anguish simmering within us. Bargaining is another stage where, in our desperation to reclaim what has been lost, we may find ourselves engaging in futile attempts to negotiate with fate or a higher power. Bargaining represents a desperate plea for a reprieve from the agony of separation, as we cling to the hope of a different outcome.

Depression is the next stage, where the depths of sorrow engulf us as we descend into the abyss of despair, grappling with overwhelming feelings of sadness, despondency, and emptiness. Depression permeates every aspect of our being, casting a shadow over even the simplest joys of life. Then, finally, comes acceptance, where it dawns like a gentle sunrise, casting its warm glow upon our weary souls. In this stage, we begin to reconcile with the permanence of our pet's absence, embracing their memory with bittersweet reverence. Acceptance does not signify the absence of pain but rather the gradual integration of loss into our lives.

Grief can make you feel like you're wandering in a maze, lost and overwhelmed. These stages we hear about are like signs pointing the way, helping us maneuver the confusing twists and turns of mourning. It's a tough journey, full of challenges, but by exploring our feelings and facing them head-on, we eventually find comfort and a way to heal.

Cognitive and Emotional Responses: Mind-Body Connection in Grief

Pet loss isn't just a rollercoaster of emotions; it's a mind–body puzzle. Grief isn't confined to our hearts; the way we think about the loss shapes how we feel it, too. It's like untangling a knot: The more we explore how our brains process what happened, the better we can understand and process the emotional turmoil.

Losing a furry friend throws a wrench into the delicate balance between how we think and how we feel. It's like trying to escape a maze in the dark. It basically feels like a tunnel filled with unexpected turns and dead ends. Grief can be a bully, shoving unwanted memories in our faces. Vivid scenes of tail wags and playful nips pop into our heads, often when we least expect them. These intrusive thoughts can be relentless, leaving us feeling ambushed by the past. On top of that, rumination, that mental hamster wheel, keeps replaying the loss over and over. We get stuck dwelling on what happened, yearning for what used to be.

Grief can also mess with our memory and focusing can be a challenge. It's like our brains become overloaded with sadness, making it hard to concentrate on anything else. Decision-making can also suffer. Simple tasks suddenly feel overwhelming, and the weight of everything can cloud our ability to make clear choices.

Emotional Reactions to Loss: The Full Spectrum of Emotions

As soon as it happens, pet loss thrusts us into a tumultuous sea of emotions, where the waves of grief crash upon the shores of our consciousness with unrestrained force. Within this maelstrom of sorrow, a kaleidoscope of feelings unfolds, each emotion reminding us of the depth of our bond with our departed companions.

Deep Sadness

At the heart of this grief lies a deep, echoing sadness. It's an emptiness that resonates with the absence of our beloved pet, a constant ache that permeates every facet of our lives. Days are filled with a heavy blanket of melancholy, a constant reminder of the loss.

Wrath and Remorse

Grief is not a monolithic entity but a multifaceted wave of emotions, crashing down with wrath and remorse. Anger may surge forth like a tempest, fueled by the unfairness of loss and the helplessness of our circumstances. Meanwhile, remorse may gnaw at the edges of our consciousness, creating wounds of regret over words unsaid and deeds undone.

The Evolution of Emotional Reactions

As we struggle to understand our grief, the intensity of our emotions ebbs and flows like the tide. The initial torrent of tears may eventually settle into a quiet ache. Moments of anger might soften, replaced by the bittersweet comfort of cherished memories. This emotional landscape is constantly changing. New waves of grief may crash over us as we confront the reality of the loss. But amid the storm, there will be moments of solace, glimpses of healing that offer us strength to weather the tempest.

The raw and complex emotions unleashed by pet loss are, in a way, a reflection of the depth of our love for our companions and the magnitude of the loss we feel. By acknowledging and embracing these emotions, no matter how difficult, we honor the complexity of our grief. This, in turn, paves the way for healing and, eventually, acceptance.

Grief Complications and Interventions

Attachment Theory and Pet Relationships

The bond between humans and their pets goes beyond the bounds of mere companionship, rooted deeply in the principles of attachment theory. Just as infants form secure attachments to their caregivers, so, too, do people build intense emotional connections with their animal companions. Just like a secure attachment with a caregiver makes a baby feel safe and loved, the bond we form with our pets provides comfort, security, and unconditional love. That's why losing a pet can feel just as devastating as losing a human family member (Earthpet, 2023).

Relevance of Attachment Theory

The central idea of attachment theory is that our patterns of attachment are shaped throughout our lives by the quality of our early relationships. When applied to pet relationships, attachment theory illuminates the nature of the human-animal bond, underscoring its role as a source of comfort, security, and unconditional love.

When a beloved pet dies, the grief can hit hard. We might feel a deep sadness, a constant longing for them, even guilt or remorse. It's all pretty similar to what people experience when they lose a close human relative. The emotions might be surprising, but they make sense when you consider how strong that pet bond can be.

Processing Grief: Personal Differences

Everyone grieves differently, and that's just as true when it comes to losing a pet. There's no right or wrong way to feel, and the path you walk will be shaped by your history, how close you were to your pet, and the ways you usually cope with sadness.

Acknowledging Personal Differences

Just as no two fingerprints are alike, our grief is like that, too. Some people form deep, secure bonds with their pets, while others might feel more detached. That's okay. The important thing is to acknowledge that your grief is real and valid, no matter how different it may seem from someone else's.

Harnessing Self-Awareness for Healing

The more you know about yourself, the better you can get through this tough time. So, take some time to think about how you typically deal with emotions and what kind of bond you had with your pet. This self-awareness can be a powerful tool for healing. By understanding your attachment style and your coping mechanisms, you can find ways to grieve that feel right for you.

The attachment theory helps explain why losing a pet can hurt so much, and understanding that everyone grieves differently shows why there's no one-size-fits-all approach to healing. The most important thing is to be kind to yourself and allow yourself to feel what you feel. There's no right or wrong way to grieve a furry, feathery, or scaly friend you loved.

Coping Strategies for Emotional Recovery

Healthy Coping Strategies

Losing a beloved pet can feel like navigating a maze of grief, filled with emotional turmoil. Regaining your footing requires strength and a toolbox of healthy coping mechanisms. By embracing practices that nurture self-compassion and emotional healing, you can find your way back to a feeling of inner peace.

Effective Coping Techniques

For emotional recovery, you'll need to develop or come up with healthy coping mechanisms that will work best for you.

Mindfulness meditation offers solace—a sanctuary of inner tranquility amid your sorrow. Through the practice of mindfulness, you can anchor yourself in the present moment, cultivating a sense of calm and equanimity in the face of emotional turbulence.

Techniques Tailored to You

There's no one-size-fits-all approach to coping with pet loss. The most effective strategies will be unique to your personality and the bond you shared with your pet.

Mindfulness Meditation

Mindfulness meditation can be a powerful tool to help you focus on the present moment, offering a sense of serenity amid the storm of emotions. Here's how to try it:

- Find a quiet place to sit comfortably.

- Close your eyes or gaze softly at a point in front of you.

- Focus on your breath, feeling the rise and fall of your chest.

- If your mind wanders, gently bring your attention back to your breath.

- Start with just a few minutes of meditation each day and gradually increase the duration as you become more comfortable.

Journaling

Journaling provides a safe space to express your thoughts, feelings, and memories without judgment. Writing down how you feel can help you untangle the complexities of grief and illuminate pathways toward healing and self-discovery. Here are some journaling prompts to get you started:

- Write a letter to your pet about the memories you shared and how you're feeling.

- Describe a happy or funny moment you had with your pet.

- What are some things you'll miss most about your pet?

Creative Expression

Art, music, or poetry can serve as powerful outlets for your emotions. These creative activities offer a way to transform pain into beauty and sorrow into strength.

- Create a piece of art that captures your pet's personality or a special memory you shared.

- Write a poem about your pet's quirks or the impact they had on your life.

- Compose a song that expresses your feelings of love and loss.

The Importance of Social Support

Remember, coping with pet loss doesn't have to be a solitary journey. So, surround yourself with supportive loved ones who understand your pain. Talking to friends, family, or even a grief counselor can provide invaluable support and validation during this difficult time.

The Healing Power of Connection

In times of profound loss, the comfort of compassionate companionship serves as a balm for the wounded soul, offering solace and understanding in the midst of despair.

- Reach out to friends and family members whom you know will be understanding and supportive.

- Consider joining a pet-loss support group where you can connect with others who have experienced similar loss.

The Therapeutic Benefits of Sharing

Shared experience can help you process your emotional healing; you can find solace and validation in the company of kindred spirits.

- Share stories and memories of your pet with loved ones.

- Look online for pet-loss forums or communities where you can connect with others who are grieving.

By embracing these healthy coping strategies and building connections with supportive communities, you can navigate grief with courage, resilience, and grace, emerging from the shadows of sorrow with newfound strength and inner peace.

Finding Light in the Darkness

Losing a pet is a heavy weight to carry. It can feel like a confusing maze of emotions, a journey from the depths of despair to slowly finding your footing again. But through it all, this experience can also prove the strength of the human spirit and the tremendous love we share with our furry companions.

Recognizing the deep sadness, anger, and even guilt we feel after losing a pet validates our grief. It's normal to grieve the loss of such a close friend. It's true that the attachment theory helps explain this deep bond—our pets provide comfort, security, and unconditional love, just like close human relationships.

There is hope, even in the midst of grief. Healthy coping mechanisms like mindfulness meditation, journaling, and creative expression can help us build inner strength and begin to heal. Talking to supportive friends, family, or even a grief counselor can also be a source of comfort and understanding. Sharing our stories and memories with others who have experienced similar loss allows us to connect with kindred spirits and find solace in their empathy.

Ultimately, working through the grief of pet loss is a personal journey. By acknowledging the emotional rollercoaster, embracing healthy coping strategies, and seeking support, we can find a way to move forward with a heart full of love for the furry friend we lost.

*****

As we bid farewell to this chapter, let us carry forward the lessons learned and the connections we've made, knowing that we are never alone in our grief. In the chapters that lie ahead, we will continue to explore the lasting legacy of our beloved pets and the joyous memories that sustain us through the darkest of times.

Chapter 6:

You Will Always Be Remembered

With Joy

Our pets aren't just companions; they weasel their way into our lives with never-ending unconditional love, playful joy, and steadfast loyalty. This grief we are feeling is about remembering and celebrating the paw prints, paw swipes, tail feathers, or fin flicks they left on our hearts. From the shared laughter to the quiet moments of affection, they've touched our souls in ways we can't even measure. So, join us as we explore all the heartwarming ways to keep the memory of our furry, feathery, or scaly friends alive, ensuring they'll always be remembered with a smile. Now, let's dive into some ideas for immortalizing the special bond you shared with your cherished companion.

Memorializing Your Beloved Pet

Creating a lasting tribute to your beloved pet can be a deeply healing part of the grieving process. Memorials offer a way to honor their memory and keep their spirit alive in your heart as well as your surroundings.

This section explores meaningful and personal ways to commemorate your pet, helping to transform your grief into a celebration of the love and joy they brought into your life.

Personalized Memorials

Just as we loved our pets the same, we memorialize them the same as we do with our human companions. Maybe we set up a picture on our desks to constantly remind ourselves of cherished moments with them, or we could put up a plaque somewhere special in their honor, or, well, there are so many ways we choose to love and honor those we lose, so why not do the same for our pets?

Planting a Living Tribute

One beautiful way to honor your pet is by planting a tree, shrub, or flower in their memory. This living tribute can serve as a constant reminder of the life you shared and the love that continues to grow even after they are gone.

The Therapeutic Value of Planting a Living Tribute

Planting a living tribute allows you to channel your grief into a positive, nurturing act. As you care for the plant, you're reminded of your pet's life and the joy they brought you. This act of planting and nurturing can be incredibly therapeutic, offering a sense of purpose and connection to your pet's memory.

Watching the tree, shrub, or flower grow and thrive symbolizes the enduring nature of your pet's spirit. Just as the plant blossoms and evolves, so, too, does your relationship with your pet's memory. It represents renewal and the continuation of life, serving as a hopeful reminder that love and memories live on, bringing comfort and peace to your heart.

By creating a personalized memorial, you not only honor your pet but also create a space of reflection and healing in your path through grief.

Memorializing Your Beloved Pet

Creating a lasting tribute to your beloved pet can be a deeply healing part of the grieving process. Memorials offer a way to honor their memory and keep their spirit alive in your heart and in your surroundings. This helps to transform your grief into a celebration of the love and joy they brought into your life.

Building a Memory Garden

Creating a dedicated memory garden is another heartfelt way to honor your beloved pet. This special space can be designed to reflect the joy and comfort your pet brought into your life, serving as a peaceful retreat where you can remember and celebrate their life.

Let's go over a few ideas for creating a specific garden space for your pet:

Personalized Plantings

- **Favorite flowers:** Plant flowers that your pet enjoyed or that remind you of them. For instance, if your dog loved running through dandelions, planting a patch of these flowers can bring back fond memories.

- **Symbolic plants:** Choose plants with symbolic meanings, such as forget-me-nots for remembrance or sunflowers for warmth and happiness.

Decorative Elements

- **Custom stones and plaques:** Engrave a stone or a plaque with your pet's name and a heartfelt message. This can serve as a centerpiece of the garden.

- **Statues and ornaments:** Place statues or garden ornaments that represent your pet or other animals, adding a whimsical and personal touch to the space.

Comforting Additions

- **Benches and seating areas:** Include a comfortable bench or seating area where you can sit and reflect. This can be a spot for meditation, reading, or simply enjoying the beauty of the garden.

- **Water features:** A small fountain or birdbath can add a soothing element to the garden, creating a tranquil atmosphere for contemplation.

The Healing Benefits of Spending Time in the Garden

Spending time in a memory garden can have many relaxing and healing benefits. Gardening itself is a therapeutic activity that helps reduce stress and anxiety. So, by tending to the garden, you're engaging in a calming routine that can soothe your mind and body. Other benefits include:

- **Connection with nature:** Being in the garden connects you with nature, promoting a sense of peace and mindfulness. The natural beauty and sounds of the garden can provide comfort and solace, making it easier for you to process your emotions.

- **A place for reflection:** The memory garden becomes a sanctuary where you can reflect on your pet's life and the special moments you shared. It offers a quiet space to grieve, remember, and celebrate your pet's memory.

- **Emotional healing:** Regular visits to the garden can help you with your grief. As you watch the plants grow and change with the seasons, you are reminded of the cycle of life and the enduring nature of love and memory.

Creating a memory garden is a meaningful way to honor your pet and provide yourself with a space of healing and tranquility. It's a living testament to the bond you shared and a place where their spirit can be remembered and cherished.

The Therapeutic Advantages of Physical Tributes

Physical tributes to a beloved pet can provide immense comfort and a tangible connection to the memories shared. These personalized keepsakes not only honor the pet's memory but also serve as a source of solace during difficult moments, helping to bridge the gap between loss and remembrance.

Creating Personalized Keepsakes

Personalized keepsakes are special items crafted to commemorate your pet. These tangible reminders can be cherished for years to come, offering a comforting presence during times of grief.

Personalized souvenirs include:

- **Engraved jewelry:** Many pet owners find comfort in wearing jewelry that bears their pet's name, a special date, or a heartfelt message. Custom-made pendants, charms, or bracelets can keep the memory of your pet close to your heart.

  - A locket containing a small photo or a snippet of fur can be another deeply personal way to carry a piece of your pet with you wherever you go.

- **Paw print impressions:** Paw print impressions made in clay or ink can capture a unique aspect of your pet. These can be framed or turned into decorative items that serve as a constant reminder of the bond you shared.

  - Some artisans create jewelry incorporating your pet's actual paw print, making for a one-of-a-kind piece that symbolizes their impact on your life. It can be a unique way to honor your pet's memory.

- **Creative artwork:** Commissioning a portrait or painting of your pet is a beautiful way to honor their memory. These artworks can capture the essence and personality of your pet, becoming a cherished part of your home.

  - Creating a photo book or a digital artwork collage can be another creative and personalized tribute. Compiling favorite photos and memories into a book can provide a tangible narrative of your pet's life and your time together.

The Comfort and Peace of Physical Memories

Having a physical memory of your pet can significantly aid in the grieving process. These keepsakes serve as constant reminders of the joy and love your pet brought into your life, helping to alleviate the feeling of emptiness that often accompanies their loss.

Physical keepsakes provide a way to maintain a tangible connection to your pet. Holding a piece of jewelry, looking at a paw print, or admiring a piece of artwork can evoke positive memories and feelings of closeness. During times of intense sadness, these mementos can offer comfort and a sense of peace. They remind you that, while your pet may no longer be physically present, their spirit and the love you shared remain with you.

Keeping these items in places where you can see them daily, like on a bedside table, a shelf, or even wearing them, offers ongoing reassurance and a reminder of the bond that endures beyond physical separation. Personalized keepsakes are not just objects; they are embodiments of the deep connection and cherished memories shared with your pet. They provide a source of comfort and healing, making your grief a little more bearable by keeping your pet's memory alive in a meaningful way.

Making a Memory Box

A memory box is another heartfelt way to preserve and celebrate the life of your beloved pet. This personalized tribute can be filled with cherished items that capture the essence of your pet and the special moments you shared. Creating a memory box offers a therapeutic and meaningful way to honor their memory, providing a tangible source of comfort and connection.

Here are a few suggestions for creating a memory box:

Choosing the Box

- **Select a special container:** Choose a box that feels significant to you. It can be a beautifully crafted wooden box, a decorative tin, or even a repurposed container that holds sentimental value.

- **Personalize it:** Decorate the box with your pet's name, photos, and any other meaningful decorations. This can be a creative and healing activity in itself.

Gathering Sentimental Items

- **Toys and accessories:** Include your pet's favorite toys. These items can evoke fond memories of the playful times you had together. Also, placing their collar or leash in the box can also serve as a powerful reminder of the bond you shared and the walks or adventures you experienced together.

- **Personal items:** If possible, add a small piece of their favorite blanket or bedding. These items carry the scent and comfort of your pet, bringing a sense of closeness. You can also include photographs that capture the essence of your pet and any artwork or drawings that you or your family created.

- **Mementos:** Place any certificates, such as adoption papers or training certificates, as well as their ID tags, into the box. These documents tell the story of your pet's life. You can also write down your favorite memories, stories, or even a letter to your pet. These written tributes can provide solace and serve as a record of the love and joy they brought into your life.

Curating the Box to Commemorate Your Pet's Existence

Let's go over a step-by-step process to do this:

1. Take some time to reflect on the special moments and unique characteristics of your pet. Think about what items truly represent your bond and the happy times you shared.

2. Collect the items you want to include in the box, ensuring each piece holds personal significance. Don't rush this process; allow yourself to feel and honor the emotions that come with it.

3. Arrange the items in a way that feels meaningful to you. You can organize them chronologically, by theme, or simply in a way that brings you comfort.

4. Consider adding personal touches, such as a small note explaining the significance of each item or a timeline of important dates and events.

5. Keep the memory box in a place where you can easily access it. This way, whenever you feel the need to connect with your pet's memory, you can open the box and find comfort in its contents. You can continue to add items to the box over time, such as new photos or mementos that remind you of your pet. This keeps the memory box an evolving tribute to their life.

Creating a memory box is not only a way to honor your pet's life but also a therapeutic activity that can aid in your grieving process. By curating a collection of meaningful items, you create a physical and emotional connection to the memories that continue to live in your heart.

Retaining a Sense of Presence

Keeping the memory of a beloved pet alive in everyday life can provide immense comfort and a sense of continuity. There are several meaningful ways to ensure that your pet's presence remains a part of your daily life, helping to ease the pain of their absence and celebrate the joy they brought to your world.

Keeping Your Pet's Memory Alive in Everyday Life

- **Displaying photos:** Dedicate a wall or a section of your home to display photos of your pet. This can include candid snapshots, professional portraits, and photos capturing special moments. You could also place framed photos around your home or create a photo album filled with your favorite images, which provides an easy way to revisit cherished memories.

- **Designating a special area in the home:** Set up a small table or shelf as a memory corner. Decorate it with your pet's photos, favorite toys, and other keepsakes. This can serve as a sacred space for reflection and remembrance. It might also be a good idea to create a personal shrine with items that were meaningful to your pet, such as their collar, a favorite blanket, or an engraved plaque. You could light a candle or add flowers to enhance the sense of tranquility and honor.

- **Incorporating memory items into daily life:** Consider jewelry or accessories that honor your pet, such as a pendant with their name or a bracelet with a paw print charm. These items keep your pet close to you at all times. You can use items like customized mugs, cushions, or blankets that feature your pet's photo or name. These small, everyday reminders can bring comfort and a smile to your face.

- **Digital tributes:** Set your phone or computer screensaver to a favorite photo of your pet. This way, you're reminded of them whenever you use your devices. Create an online memorial page or social media tribute where you can share memories, photos, and stories. It allows for an interactive way to keep the memory alive and connect with others who knew and loved your pet.

The Comfort of Knowing Your Pet Is Still Present Through These Reminders

Having visual and tangible reminders of your pet around the home helps maintain a sense of their presence. This continuity can be deeply comforting, as it bridges the gap between their physical absence and the emotional bond you still share. Then, engaging with these reminders in your daily routine can create moments of connection. Whether it's seeing their photo in the morning or wearing a piece of jewelry that honors them, these interactions can provide solace and a sense of closeness.

The loss of a pet often leads to feelings of loneliness. Having reminders around can mitigate this by providing a sense of companionship and ongoing presence. These reminders can also serve as a way for you to process your grief. Reflecting on the positive memories and the joy your pet brought into your life can be a healing experience.

By integrating these practices into your life, you create a lasting tribute to your pet that honors their memory and the special bond you shared. These reminders not only keep their presence alive but also offer comfort and support during the grieving process.

Sharing Their Legacy With Others

Sharing the legacy of your beloved pet can be a powerful way to honor their memory and keep their spirit alive. By commemorating their life and the joy they brought, you can connect with others who understand your grief and celebrate the special bond you shared. Following are some meaningful ways to share your pet's legacy with others.

Create a Digital Memorial

Creating an online memorial or tribute page for your pet is a beautiful way to preserve and share their story. It allows you to compile and present memories in a format that is easily accessible to friends, family, and a wider community of animal lovers.

Ideas for Creating an Online Memorial or Tribute Page

- **Choose a platform:** There are numerous websites specifically designed for creating pet memorials, like ILovedMyPet.com, everloved.com, Critters.com, Pet-Loss.net, and PetsMattered Online Memorials for free pet memorials at https://pets.youmattered.com. These platforms often provide templates and tools to help you easily set up a tribute page. Platforms like Facebook, Instagram, and even dedicated groups on sites like Reddit can also be used to share your pet's story with a broad audience.

- **Compile content:** You can then upload a collection of your favorite photos and videos of your pet. Capture moments from their everyday lives, special occasions, and their unique quirks and personalities.

- **Stories and memories:** Share heartfelt stories and anecdotes that highlight the special moments you shared with your pet. This could include tales of their antics, their comforting presence, and how they impacted your life.

- **Interactive elements:** You could include a guestbook where friends and family can leave messages, share their memories, and offer condolences. You could enable comments or reactions on photos and posts, allowing others to engage with your pet's story and express their support.

The Accessibility and Reach of Internet Memorials

Connecting With a Wider Community

Online memorials can reach a global audience, allowing you to connect with people who have experienced similar losses and understand the depth of your grief.

Many pet owners have found solace and support in online communities. So, by sharing your pet's story, this can help you find empathetic listeners and friends who offer comfort and understanding.

Preservation of Memories

Digital memorials ensure that your pet's memory is preserved for years to come. Unlike physical mementos, which can be lost or damaged, online tributes remain accessible and intact.

Friends and family can visit the memorial at any time, from anywhere, providing ongoing support and connection.

Celebrating Life

An online memorial allows you to focus on celebrating your pet's life rather than just mourning their loss. By sharing their story and the joy they brought, you keep their spirit alive and honor their legacy in a meaningful way.

Then, too, creating and sharing a digital memorial can be a cathartic process, providing a space to grieve, remember, and celebrate your pet's life. It connects you with a community of fellow pet lovers and ensures that your beloved companion is remembered and cherished forever.

Donating or Volunteering in Their Honor

Another great way to honor your pet's memory is through acts of kindness and generosity, which can provide you with a sense of purpose and fulfillment during the grieving process. Making donations or volunteering in their name not only respects their memory but also helps other animals in need, continuing the legacy of love and compassion your pet brought into your life.

Ideas for Making Philanthropic Contributions

Donations to Animal Welfare Organizations

You could consider making a financial contribution to organizations that work toward animal rescue, rehabilitation, and welfare. This could include local shelters, national animal protection groups, or specific causes like wildlife conservation. Many shelters and rescues appreciate donations of supplies such as pet food, toys, bedding, and medical supplies. These contributions can directly impact the well-being of animals in their care.

Fundraising Efforts

You could set up a crowdfunding campaign in your pet's name to raise money for a cause they would have loved. This could be anything from supporting a local shelter to funding medical care for stray animals.

Another great idea is to set up or establish a memorial fund where friends and family can contribute. The collected funds can then be donated to an animal charity of your choice.

Volunteering at Shelters

When it comes to charity, you may not be able to stop yourself from giving some hands-on assistance. You can always offer some time at a local animal shelter. Volunteering activities might include walking dogs, socializing cats, assisting with adoption events, or helping with administrative tasks.

You could also temporarily foster animals in your home until they find permanent homes. This provides them with a safe and loving environment, mirroring the care you provided your pet.

You can also get involved in educational outreach programs that teach the community about responsible pet ownership and the importance of animal welfare. You can advocate for animal rights and welfare in your community. This could include participating in events, signing petitions, and spreading awareness through social media.

Respecting Their Memory Through Giving Back

By giving back in your pet's name, you honor their spirit of love and compassion. Every act of kindness you perform is a testament to the bond you shared and the positive impact they had on your life. Another beneficial part of engaging in charitable activities is that it can be incredibly healing. It provides a way to channel your grief into positive action, helping you cope with loss while making a difference in the lives of other animals.

Aside from this, your contributions help improve the lives of countless animals, creating a lasting legacy for your pet. The joy and comfort they brought you can now extend to others, perpetuating their memory in a meaningful way.

Through volunteering and donating, you become part of a community of animal lovers and advocates. This sense of belonging and shared purpose can provide additional support and comfort while you are grieving.

By donating or volunteering in your pet's honor, you transform your grief into a powerful force for good. This not only respects their memory but also ensures that their legacy of love and compassion continues to make a positive impact on the world.

*****

Honoring the memory of your beloved pet is a vital part of the healing process. Through personalized memorials, physical tributes, and acts of charity, you can keep their spirit alive and find comfort in your grief journey. Whether it's planting a tree, creating a memory garden, or volunteering in their name, these meaningful gestures offer solace and a sense of continuity. Remembering your pet with joy and love helps to transform your sadness into a celebration of the life you shared.

Now, as you continue to navigate the grieving process, it's essential to recognize the impact that community support can have on your emotional well-being. In the next chapter, we'll explore the healing power of connecting with others who understand your loss. From joining pet-loss support groups to sharing your experiences with empathetic friends and family, we'll explore how community support can offer comfort, validation, and a sense of belonging during this difficult time.

Chapter 7:

The Healing Power of Community

Support

Grieving the loss of a beloved pet is a deeply personal experience, yet it is also one that can be greatly influenced by the support of others. The power of community support during times of loss cannot be underestimated. Whether it's through friends, family, or pet-loss support groups, having a network of empathetic people can provide comfort, validation, and understanding. In this chapter, we will explore the significance of these support networks and how they can help you come to terms with the complex emotions that come with bereavement. By connecting with others who understand your pain, you can find solace and strength on your journey toward healing.

The Role of Support Networks

Community support plays a very important role in the grieving process. Whether through friends, family, or specialized support groups, being surrounded by others who understand and empathize with your pain can provide immense comfort. Some of the most beneficial forms of community support are pet-loss support groups. These groups offer a safe space where you can share your experiences, express your emotions, and receive understanding and empathy from others who have gone through similar losses. In this section, we will explore the benefits of participating in both in-person and online pet loss support groups.

Benefits of Pet-Loss Support Groups

In-Person Support Groups

Participating in local pet-loss support groups can be an immensely healing experience. These groups provide face-to-face interaction and the opportunity to form meaningful connections with others who understand your grief.

- **Shared experiences:** In-person support groups allow you to share your story and hear others' stories as well. This mutual exchange of experiences can be incredibly validating and comforting, helping you feel less alone in your grief.

- **Emotional support:** Group gatherings provide a safe environment where you can openly express your emotions without fear of judgment. The empathy and understanding you receive from fellow group members can be a source of great comfort.

- **Practical advice:** Members of support groups often share coping strategies and practical advice on how to navigate the grieving process. This collective wisdom can offer new perspectives and helpful tools to manage your grief.

- **Sense of community:** Being part of a group that meets regularly can create a sense of community and belonging. Consistent support and connection with others who have experienced similar losses can be a powerful aid in your healing process.

In-person support groups not only provide emotional solace but also create a sense of community that can significantly aid in the grieving process. By participating in these gatherings, you can find empathy, understanding, and practical advice from others who genuinely comprehend the pain of losing a cherished pet.

Benefits of Pet-Loss Support Groups: Online Community and Forums

In addition to in-person support groups, online communities and forums offer a valuable resource for those grieving the loss of a pet. These platforms provide a space where people can connect with others from around the world who understand the unique challenges and heartache that come with pet loss.

- **Simplicity and accessibility:** Online support groups are easy to access from the comfort of your home. This convenience means you can seek support whenever you need it, without the constraints of meeting times or locations.

- **Anonymity and comfort:** For those who may feel uncomfortable sharing their grief in person, online forums provide a degree of anonymity, which can make it easier to express your emotions and experiences openly.

- **Diverse perspectives:** Online communities bring together a diverse group of people from different backgrounds and cultures. This diversity can provide a broader range of experiences and coping strategies, offering fresh insights and perspectives on grief.

- **Constant support:** Online groups are available 24/7, providing continuous support. Whether you're struggling late at night or early in the morning, there's always someone who can offer a kind word or empathetic ear.

By participating in online pet-bereavement support groups, you can connect with a global community that understands the specific grief of losing a pet. These forums offer not only practical advice and emotional support but also a sense of belonging to a wider network of people who share your pain and can help you in your healing journey.

Shared Experiences and Comfort in Stories

In the grieving process, finding solace in shared experiences and stories can be incredibly therapeutic. When we share our memories and hear those of others, we create a sense of community and mutual understanding that helps us feel less alone in our sorrow.

Storytelling and Healing

Sharing the stories of our beloved pets and the joy they brought into our lives can be a powerful tool for healing. Whether it's recounting a favorite memory, describing a cherished routine, or simply expressing the depth of our loss, storytelling allows us to process our emotions and honor our pets' lives.

- **Therapeutic value:** Telling our pets' stories can serve as a form of therapy. It helps us articulate our grief, recognize the love and joy our pets brought into our lives, and acknowledge the pain of their absence. This process can be cathartic, helping to release pent-up emotions and providing a way to make sense of our loss.

- **Validation and comfort:** Hearing the experiences of other pet owners can offer validation for our feelings. Knowing that others have gone through similar experiences can be immensely comforting. It reassures us that our grief is normal and that we are not alone in our pain.

- **Sense of connection:** Storytelling creates a bond between people who have experienced the loss of a pet. Sharing memories and listening to others' tales builds a sense of connection and community. This shared understanding can help alleviate feelings of isolation and provide emotional support during a difficult time.

By engaging in storytelling, either by sharing your own experiences or listening to those of others, you can find comfort and a sense of belonging. This exchange of stories helps to affirm the special bond you had with your pet and reminds you that your grief is shared by many who understand and empathize with your loss.

Finding Common Ground

In times of grief, finding common ground with others who have experienced similar losses can provide immense comfort and understanding. By connecting with people who share in the pain of pet loss, we create a supportive network that validates our feelings and helps us all work through our grief together.

Encouraging Shared Experiences

Reaching out to others who have walked a similar path of pet loss can be a powerful source of solace. Here are some ways to connect with people who understand your grief:

- **Join support groups:** Seek out local or online pet-loss support groups where you can connect with others who are also grieving the loss of their beloved companions. These groups provide a safe space to share your experiences, receive empathy, and offer support to fellow members.

- **Attend pet-loss memorials or events:** Participate in memorial services or events organized in honor of pets. These gatherings bring together people who share a common bond of love for animals, fostering connections and understanding among attendees.

- **Reach out to friends and family:** Don't hesitate to lean on friends and family members who have also experienced the loss of a pet. Even if they haven't gone through the same situation, their empathy and support can still provide immense comfort.

Consolation in Shared Understanding

Finding common ground with others who have suffered pet loss offers a sense of consolation and reassurance:

- **Validation of feelings:** Connecting with others who have experienced similar losses validates your feelings of grief.

Knowing that your emotions are understood and accepted by others helps alleviate feelings of isolation and loneliness.

- **Shared coping strategies:** By sharing experiences and coping strategies with others, you can gain valuable insights and support. Learning how others have managed their grief can provide inspiration and guidance as you find your path toward healing.

- **Building a support network:** Establishing connections with fellow pet owners who understand your pain creates a supportive network that you can lean on during difficult times. Knowing that you have a community of understanding people to turn to can offer comfort and strength throughout your mourning process.

In seeking common ground with others who have experienced pet loss, you can find solace in the shared understanding and empathy of those who truly comprehend the depth of your sorrow. By connecting with fellow mourners, you build a network of support that helps you navigate the challenges of grief with compassion and understanding.

Seeking Support From Friends and Family

During times of grief, the support of friends and family plays a very important role in overcoming the emotional challenges of pet loss. Let's look at the significance of this support network and how it can aid in the healing process.

The Role of Family and Friends in Grief

Friends and family members often serve as pillars of strength and sources of comfort during times of sorrow. Here's how their support can contribute to your healing:

- **Emotional support:** Loved ones can offer a listening ear and a shoulder to lean on as you navigate the complex emotions of pet loss. Their presence provides reassurance that you're not alone in your grief and that your feelings are valid and understood.

- **Practical assistance:** Friends and family members can offer practical assistance with tasks, such as arranging memorial services, handling logistical matters, or simply providing companionship during difficult moments. Their willingness to lend a helping hand alleviates some of the burdens associated with grieving.

- **Validation of feelings:** When you share your emotions with friends and family, they validate your feelings and provide empathy and understanding. Knowing that your loved ones acknowledge the depth of your sorrow can bring you a sense of validation.

Experiencing Grief Together

- Encourage open and honest communication with your loved ones about your grief. Expressing your thoughts and feelings allows them to better understand your needs and offer support accordingly.

- Be open to accepting support from friends and family, even if it feels uncomfortable at times. Allowing yourself to lean on others for support is a sign of strength, not weakness.

- Remember that supporting one another goes both ways. While you may be grieving the loss of your pet, your friends and family members may also be experiencing their feelings of sadness. Being there for one another creates a reciprocal cycle of support and healing.

In seeking support from friends and family, you can find comfort in the shared love and understanding of those closest to you. Their presence, empathy, and practical assistance offer invaluable support as you deal with the challenges of pet loss and grief.

Practical Assistance and Care

When grieving the loss of a beloved pet, practical assistance and care from friends and family can make a significant difference. Let's explore how their support extends beyond emotional comfort to encompass practical help and care.

Extending a Helping Hand

Friends and family members offer assistance with everyday tasks that might feel overwhelming during times of grief. Whether it's running errands, preparing meals, or handling household chores, their willingness to lend a helping hand lightens your load and allows you to focus on self-care.

For those with remaining pets, friends and family step in to provide care and companionship to furry family members. Whether it's feeding, walking, or simply offering comfort to other pets grieving the loss of their companion, their support ensures that all members of the family receive the attention they need.

The Relief of Supportive Care

By shouldering some of the responsibilities and tasks that come with daily life, friends and family members alleviate stress and provide much-needed relief. Their practical assistance allows you to work through your grief without feeling overwhelmed by the demands of daily life. Knowing that you have a support system of friends and family to rely on brings a sense of reassurance and comfort. Their willingness to step in and offer assistance demonstrates their commitment to your well-being and serves as a reminder that you are not alone.

In times of pet loss, the practical assistance and care provided by friends and family members serve as pillars of support, offering relief from the burdens of daily life and ensuring that you can focus on your healing process. Their willingness to extend a helping hand underscores the strength of your support network and reinforces the bonds of love and friendship that sustain you through difficult times.

Effective Communication Regarding Grief Needs

Navigating grief requires open and honest communication with friends and family about your mourning needs. Let's explore how you can express your needs effectively during this challenging time.

Expressing Grief Needs Effectively

- Encourage open dialogue with your loved ones about your needs. Express your feelings, concerns, and preferences openly, allowing them to understand the support you require during this difficult period.

- Be honest and vulnerable about your emotions and challenges. Share your thoughts and feelings authentically, allowing your loved ones to provide meaningful support and understanding.

- Recognize the importance of setting boundaries when necessary. Communicate your boundaries clearly and assertively, ensuring that your needs are respected and honored by those around you.

- Don't hesitate to ask for assistance when needed. Whether it's practical help with daily tasks or emotional support during moments of distress, communicate your specific needs to your friends and family members.

- Offer guidance to your loved ones on how they can best support you. Provide suggestions and recommendations based on your preferences, helping them understand the type of assistance and care that would be most beneficial to you.

By fostering open communication and expressing your grief needs effectively, you create a supportive environment where your loved ones can offer meaningful assistance and understanding.

Creating Rituals of Remembrance

In times of loss, creating rituals of remembrance can be incredibly healing for both pet owners who experienced loss and their families. Let's explore the therapeutic benefits of these rituals and how they can help you celebrate the memory of a beloved pet.

Therapeutic Benefits

Rituals of remembrance provide an opportunity to honor the memory of a cherished pet in a meaningful and tangible way. They allow family members and friends to come together to pay tribute to the life and love shared with their furry companion.

Engaging in rituals can offer a sense of closure and acceptance following the loss of a pet. They provide a structured framework for processing grief and saying goodbye, allowing people to find comfort and solace in shared experiences.

Rituals of remembrance offer a space for people to connect with their emotions and with each other. They provide a supportive environment for sharing stories, expressing feelings, and finding solace in the company of loved ones.

Personalized Tributes

We have looked at these before, but some other ideas include:

- **Memorial plaques and artwork:** Encourage friends and family to create personalized tributes, such as memorial plaques or artwork, honoring the pet's memory. These tangible reminders can serve as symbols of love and remembrance, providing comfort and solace in times of sorrow.

- **Collaborative activities:** Collaborative activities, such as planting a tree together or releasing sky lanterns, can enhance a sense of connection and shared memory among family members and friends. These meaningful gestures allow people to come together in solidarity and support, strengthening bonds and fostering healing.

By creating rituals of remembrance and encouraging personalized tributes, friends and family can come together to honor the life and legacy of a beloved pet. These rituals provide a space for healing, connection, and celebration of the special bond shared with their furry companion.

Building a Supportive Network

During intense moments of grief, having a supportive network can make all the difference. Let's explore how you can build friendships and connections with other pet owners to find comfort and understanding outside the context of mourning. This is why you'll need to seek out a supportive network if you don't already have one.

Encouraging Connections

You can seek out friendships with other pet owners based on shared interests and activities. Whether it's attending dog parks, joining pet-related clubs, or using online forums, finding common ground can lay the foundation for meaningful connections.

- There is value that comes from volunteering at animal shelters or participating in pet-related community activities. These opportunities not only allow you to give back to the community but also provide avenues for meeting like-minded people who share a passion for animals.

- You can speak to friends and family, in particular those who are also pet owners or pet lovers. This can strengthen bonds with those close to us who understand the pain of pet loss.

- You could also go online and find support groups on social media sites like Facebook.

These ideas can give you a starting point, and once you take the first step, finding a supportive company will become easier.

Benefits of a Supportive Network

- **Shared understanding:** Building connections with other pet owners provides a sense of camaraderie and a shared understanding. It creates a supportive environment where you can freely express your feelings and experiences without fear of judgment.

- **Emotional support:** Having a supportive network offers emotional support and validation during times of grief. Friends and fellow pet owners can offer empathy, compassion, and practical advice, helping you better understand what you are going through with mourning.

Finding Purpose and Connection

Engaging in pet-related community activities can create a sense of purpose and connection. Whether it's organizing fundraisers for animal charities or participating in pet adoption events, giving back to the community can provide a sense of fulfillment and belonging.

By building friendships and connections with other pet owners, you can strengthen your social bonds and expand your support network. These relationships offer a sense of companionship and solidarity, enhancing overall well-being.

So, build a supportive network with other pet owners. This can provide invaluable comfort, understanding, and companionship during times of grief. By seeking out shared interests, engaging in community involvement, and building meaningful connections, you can find solace and strength in the company of others who share their love for animals.

*****

In this chapter, we've explored the impact of building a supportive network while experiencing pet-loss grief. By building connections with other pet owners, you can find solace, understanding, and companionship outside the context of mourning. Whether through shared interests, community involvement, or volunteering, these relationships offer emotional support, validation, and a sense of purpose. As you continue to seek out meaningful connections and build supportive networks, you will discover the invaluable comfort and strength that come from walking this path together.

In Chapter 8, we'll explore the process of finding joy and healing after pet loss. Through reflection, strength of character, and the power of positivity, pet owners who have experienced loss will learn how to embrace life's moments of happiness and reclaim their sense of joy amid the pain of grief. Join us as we uncover the journey of healing and discover the boundless possibilities of joy awaiting on the road ahead.

Chapter 8:

Finding Joy Again

In the aftermath of pet loss, the prospect of rediscovering joy may seem distant and uncertain. Yet, as we work through our grief, we often find that healing and happiness can coexist. In this chapter, we'll explore the positive effects of resilience, positivity, and connection as we move through the path toward finding joy once more. By embracing new experiences, building meaningful connections, and honoring our beloved pets' legacies, we'll uncover the beauty of life's moments and rediscover the joy that resides within our hearts. Join us as we embark on a journey of healing, hope, and the boundless possibilities of joy awaiting us on the road ahead.

Embracing New Possibilities

In the wake of pet loss, the notion of welcoming a new furry companion into our lives can evoke a whirlwind of emotions. While the pain of loss may still linger, the idea of opening our hearts to a new pet offers a glimmer of hope and the healing potential. However, it's essential to recognize and go through the mixed emotions that accompany this decision.

Exploring the Concept of Accepting a New Pet

Considering the prospect of adopting a new pet after a loss can be a complex and emotional journey. It's natural to experience a range of conflicting emotions, from apprehension and guilt to hope and excitement. These mixed feelings are only further proof of the deep bond we shared with our previous pet and the significance of their absence in our lives.

Understanding Mixed Emotions

As we think of the possibility of bringing a new pet into our homes, it's not uncommon to grapple with various feelings of shame and guilt. We may even question whether it's too soon to move on or worry that we're betraying the memory of our beloved companion. Additionally, the fear of comparison—comparing a new pet with the one we've lost—can weigh heavily on our minds, creating a barrier to embracing new possibilities. This is natural.

However, amid these complex emotions, there's a yearning for companionship and the comfort that a new pet can provide. Despite the uncertainty, there's a flicker of hope—a belief that welcoming a new pet into our lives can be a source of joy and healing, a desire to fill the void our beloved pets have left behind.

For me, the prospect of opening my heart to a new pet was met with a whirlwind of emotions in the beginning. After losing my cherished companions, I grappled with feelings of guilt and uncertainty. Would I be able to love another pet as deeply as I had loved my previous ones? Would I be doing a disservice to their memory by welcoming a new furry friend into my life? Was I a good person for even thinking of getting another pet after I lost two of my trusted friends? It was a terrible experience but, admittedly, one that I had to go through.

However, as time passed and I reflected on the joy and companionship that pets had brought me in the past, I began to entertain the idea of adopting a new pet. Despite the lingering sadness, I found solace in the thought of providing a loving home to an animal in need. And so, with a mix of apprehension and hope, I am embarking on the journey of welcoming a new pet into my life—a decision that will ultimately lead to moments of joy, laughter, and renewed companionship. I did think about it for quite some time and decided that I would need to visit my local pet shelter to get the process started. I haven't adopted a new pet as yet, as I am waiting for the right little companion—one who I know needs me and vice versa.

This is another point to keep in mind. When you lose a pet, you shouldn't rush to adopt a new one in the hopes that this will ease some of the pain. Yes, it can distract you but never allowing yourself to fully heal and get through the grief, will only cause you some deeper heartache down the road. So, I advise that you experience the grief and sorrow that comes with pet loss. Wait until your heart is ready, then move on when you are ready and find the perfect pet who needs you just as much as you need them.

Now, let's move deeper into the process of embracing new possibilities and welcoming a new pet into our lives after a loss.

The Healing Power of Animal Companionship

As we've already seen, adopting a new pet can come with its fair share of possibilities.

Studies have shown that the presence of a pet can have an impact on our mental and emotional well-being. From reducing stress and anxiety to promoting feelings of happiness and belonging, the bond between humans and animals is a source of immeasurable comfort and support. The unconditional love and companionship offered by a new pet can serve as a guiding light in our journey of healing, providing solace and companionship during times of sadness and grief (*The power of pets*, 2018).

Let's dive into the process of getting a new pet after losing a loved one.

Preparing for a New Furry Companion

Before welcoming a new pet into our homes, it's very important to consider the timing and readiness for this significant step. Selecting the right time to bring a new pet into our lives involves careful reflection and consideration of our emotional readiness and practical obligations.

Selecting the Right Time

Deciding when to bring a new pet into our home requires thoughtful consideration of our emotional state and readiness to open our hearts to a new furry friend. While the desire for companionship and healing may be strong, we need to allow ourselves the necessary time to process our loss fully. Rushing into adopting a new pet before we're emotionally prepared may hinder the healing process and create additional stress for both us and the new pet. There is also the disadvantage that you may not be able to fully bond with or accept the new pet, as feelings of loss and grief hold you back.

Instead, you should take the time to grieve and reflect on your feelings before making the decision to adopt a new pet. By honoring your emotions and allowing yourself the space to heal, you can ensure that you're ready to provide the love and care that a new pet deserves. Additionally, considering the practical responsibilities of pet ownership, such as financial obligations and time commitments, is essential to ensuring a smooth transition for both you and your new furry companion.

Now, let's take a turn and move deeper into the process of preparing for a new furry companion with practical advice on welcoming a new pet into our lives with love and compassion.

Finding the Perfect Match

As we go on that exciting, yet sad, quest of welcoming a new pet into our lives, finding the perfect match is essential for building a harmonious and fulfilling relationship. While the prospect of adopting a new furry companion brings excitement and anticipation, it's very important to consider various factors to ensure compatibility and a successful bond. Now, let's go over the key factors to keep in mind while selecting a new pet and the advantages of adopting from shelters or rescue organizations.

Factors to Consider

When selecting a new pet, you need to consider various factors that align with your lifestyle, energy levels, and preferences. This is especially true if you're trying to get a different type of pet, like moving from a cat to a dog, and so on. Here are some key points to keep in mind:

- **Living environment:** Do you live in an apartment or a house with a yard? Consider the space available for your pet to move around comfortably. Some pets, like larger dogs, might need more space to roam and play, while others, like cats or small dogs, might be more adaptable to smaller living areas.

- **Daily routine:** How much time do you spend at home versus time spent away? Pets require time and attention, so think about your daily schedule now that you've lost a pet, and how the new pet will fit into it. If you have a busy lifestyle, a pet that is more independent or requires less constant interaction might be a better fit.

- **Available space for activities:** Assess the amount of space you have for the pet's activities and exercise. Larger breeds or high-energy pets will need ample room to play and exercise.

- **Exercise requirements:** Different pets have different exercise needs. Consider how much time you can commit to walking, playing, and exercising your pet each day. High-energy breeds will need more physical activity, while others may be content with shorter play sessions.

- **Grooming needs:** Some pets require regular grooming, while others have low-maintenance coats. Think about whether you have the time and resources for frequent grooming appointments or if a pet with minimal grooming needs suits you and your lifestyle better.

- **Temperament:** Consider the temperament and personality traits of the pet. Some pets are more social and outgoing, while others are shy or reserved. Ensure the pet's temperament aligns with your personality and lifestyle.

- **Compatibility with other pets:** If you still have other pets, think about how a new pet will fit into the existing dynamic. Some pets get along well with others, while others may prefer to be the only animal in the home.

- **Allergies:** Check if anyone in your household has allergies to certain types of animals. Hypoallergenic breeds might be a good option if allergies are a concern.

- **Lifespan and commitment:** Now, for the most important part, consider the lifespan of the pet and your long-term commitment. Ensure you're ready for the years of care ahead.

By carefully considering these factors, you can find a pet that not only fits seamlessly into your life but also brings joy and companionship to your home. This thoughtful approach helps ensure a successful match and a harmonious relationship with your new furry friend.

Advantages of Adoption

Adopting a pet from shelters or rescue organizations offers numerous advantages, both for the pet and you, the adopter. By adopting from a shelter, you have the opportunity to give a needy pet a second chance at life and provide them with a loving and caring home. Many shelter pets are eager to form a bond with their new owners and bring joy and companionship into their lives.

Furthermore, adopting from shelters or rescue organizations often comes with added benefits such as vaccinations, spaying or neutering, and microchipping, reducing the initial expenses associated with pet ownership. Additionally, by adopting from shelters, you'll contribute to the ongoing efforts to reduce pet overpopulation and support the welfare of animals in need.

By going over the advantages you're providing, and not just to yourself by adopting them, you'll recognize that it may just give you what you need. Then, through careful consideration and informed decision-making, you can ensure that you find the perfect furry companion to enrich your life and bring you joy and companionship in the years to come.

Discovering New Passions and Interests After Pet Loss

As we move through the journey of healing and rediscovery after the loss of a beloved pet, embracing new passions and interests can be a powerful avenue for finding joy and solace. You may not want to get another pet, but you would like to find something to do that can help in your recovery. This is not an issue, and many have gone this route. After all, for some of us, opening our hearts to love after loss may not be the best thing.

Now, let's explore the therapeutic benefits of engaging in creative activities, connecting with nature, and pursuing hobbies that ignite a sense of wonder, help in the healing journey.

Exploring Creative Activities

Creative expression offers an outlet for processing emotions, building self-discovery and finding healing amid grief. Exploring various creative pursuits can provide a channel for expressing complex feelings and capturing cherished memories.

Creative ideas to take part in include:

Painting and Drawing

Pick up some paint, brushes, and a canvas, or simply a sketchpad and pencils. Let your emotions flow through your art. Whether it's abstract shapes or detailed portraits, the act of creating can be incredibly therapeutic.

Paint or draw your favorite memories of your pet. Capture moments that brought you joy and made you smile. This can be a wonderful way to keep their spirit alive.

Journaling

Journaling is a powerful way to process grief. Write down your thoughts, feelings, and memories without any pressure of structure or grammar. Let the words flow naturally.

You can create a dedicated journal for your pet. Fill it with stories, photos, and reflections. Include moments that were special to you and your pet.

Photography

Spend time outdoors, taking photographs of landscapes, flowers, or anything that brings you peace. Nature can be incredibly soothing and can help you feel connected to the world around you.

You can create a collage of your pet's photos. Arrange them in a way that tells the story of your time together. You can frame it or keep it in a special album.

Crafting

Gather pictures, letters, and mementos of your pet and create a scrapbook. Decorate it with stickers, ribbons, and other embellishments to make it uniquely yours.

You can make something tangible to remember your pet by. This could be a quilt made from their favorite blankets, a piece of jewelry with their paw print, or a decorated memory box.

Music and Sound

You can compile playlists of music that remind you of your pet. These could be songs that calm you or tunes that you used to play while spending time together.

If you've always wanted to learn an instrument, now might be a good time. Music can be a powerful emotional outlet and a way to express what words cannot.

Writing Letters

You can write letters to your pet as if they were still here. Share your day, your thoughts, and how much you miss them. This can be a comforting way to maintain a connection.

You can write stories or poems about your pet. Let your imagination flow and create tales that celebrate their life and the joy they brought you.

Gardening

You can create a special garden in your pet's honor. Plant flowers, shrubs, or even a tree. Spend time tending to it, and let it be a living tribute to your beloved pet. You can also include personalized items like engraved stones, wind chimes, or garden statues to make the space uniquely meaningful.

Cooking and Baking

If your pet had a favorite treat, bake a batch in their honor. Share them with other pet owners or donate them to a local animal shelter.

You could also cook for comfort, preparing meals that make you feel better. Cooking can be a meditative process and a way to nurture yourself during difficult times.

Mindfulness and Meditation

You can use guided meditation apps or videos that focus on grief and healing. This can help you center your thoughts and find inner peace. Or follow this simple guide:

- Choose a peaceful, comfortable spot where you won't be disturbed.

- Start with a short session, such as 5–10 minutes, and gradually increase as you become more comfortable.

- Sit in a comfortable position with your back straight. You can sit on a chair or on the floor with a cushion.

- Gently close your eyes to help minimize distractions and focus inward.

- Take deep breaths in and out. Pay attention to the sensation of the air entering and leaving your body.

- Allow yourself to feel the sadness and loss. Acknowledge these emotions without judgment.

- You can silently repeat a comforting word or phrase, such as "peace" or "I am healing," to help maintain focus.

- Picture happy memories with your pet. Imagine them in a peaceful place, feeling content and happy.

- Remind yourself that it's okay to grieve. Be kind and gentle with yourself during this time.

- Before concluding, take a moment to reflect on the joy and love your pet brought into your life. Feel grateful for the time you had together.

- Slowly bring your awareness back to the present moment. Open your eyes and take a few deep breaths before moving on with your day.

Regular practice of this meditation can help you process your grief and find moments of peace amid the sorrow.

Breathing Exercises

Practice deep breathing exercises to help calm your mind and body. Focus on your breath and allow yourself to release tension and stress from your mind and body, all while keeping your eyes closed.

Embracing Nature's Healing Potential

Nature has long been recognized for its healing properties, offering solace, tranquility, and a sense of renewal to those who seek it. Immersing yourself in outdoor activities such as hiking, gardening, and birdwatching can provide a welcome respite from the challenges of grief and loss.

Engaging with the natural world allows us to reconnect with the rhythms of life, find solace in the beauty of the natural landscape, and gain perspective on the cycle of life and renewal. Whether tending to a garden, going on a scenic hike, or simply observing the birds in flight, connecting with nature can instill a sense of peace, serenity, and hope while healing.

The bottom line is that there is power to be gained from creative expression and outdoor activities. And, through embracing new passions and interests, we can honor our pet's memory, nurture our well-being, and take steps toward healing and renewal.

Connecting With Others Through Shared Interests

In times of grief, finding companionship and support among those who share our passions and interests can be immensely comforting and uplifting.

By actively engaging in clubs or groups related to our interests, we open ourselves up to the possibility of forging new friendships and connections that help us move beyond our grief. These shared interests serve as a foundation for meaningful interactions and conversations, providing a sense of camaraderie and understanding as we heal.

Participating in workshops or skill-building activities related to our hobbies not only expands our knowledge and abilities but also offers a sense of accomplishment and growth. Whether learning a new skill, honing existing talents, or simply immersing ourselves in the joy of shared experiences, these opportunities for personal development contribute to our overall sense of well-being and fulfillment.

As we embrace the journey of rediscovery and joy, let us seek out opportunities to connect with others who share our passions, interests, and aspirations. Through the bonds we create in shared experiences and the support of like-minded individuals, we can find solace, companionship, and a renewed sense of purpose as we begin to heal.

Moving Forward

As we explore the delicate balance between mourning our loss and embracing the promise of new beginnings, it's important to approach the transition period with a sense of mindfulness and introspection. This phase marks a significant milestone in our healing process—a time when the weight of grief begins to lighten, and the prospect of new possibilities beckons.

Approaching the Transition Period

In this phase, it's natural to experience a complex interplay of emotions as we bid farewell to the past and tentatively step into the future. While the pain of loss may still linger, it coexists alongside feelings of anticipation, hope, and excitement for what lies ahead.

As we go through this transition and heal further, it's important to find meaningful ways to commemorate the past while embracing the present and future. Honoring the memory of our beloved pet through rituals, memorials, or acts of remembrance allows us to pay tribute to their legacy while acknowledging our readiness to move forward.

Amid the flow of emotions, cultivating patience and self-compassion becomes paramount. Recognizing that healing is not a linear process but rather a series of ebbs and flows, we grant ourselves the grace to move through the intricacies of sorrow and regeneration at our own pace. By extending kindness and understanding to ourselves, we create space for growth, resilience, and self-discovery.

Acknowledging Milestones of Healing

As we move along the winding path of grief and renewal, it's very important to recognize and celebrate the milestones of healing that mark our journey. Each moment of joy, laughter, and tranquility serves as a poignant reminder of our capacity to find light amid the darkness of loss.

It can be easy to overlook the sense of thankfulness that lies within us—a gratitude born from the love and memories we shared with our departed pet. As we reflect on the cherished moments and precious bonds that defined our companionship, we cultivate a deep sense of gratitude for the blessings they had on our lives. In this spirit of gratitude, we find solace, acceptance, and a renewed appreciation for the love that continues to grow within our hearts.

*****

As we bid farewell to this chapter and start to move forward, let's embrace the transitions with open hearts and open minds, trusting in the resilience of the human spirit and the tremendous power of healing, allowing us to see and embrace life's beauty again. With each step we take, may we find solace in the memories of the past, strength in the challenges of the present, and hope in the promise of the future.

Conclusion

As we reach the end of this book, let's take a brief moment to reflect on what we have learned, and to recognize just how far you've come with your grief.

Throughout this book, we've explored the emotions and sorrow that come with losing a beloved pet. We've learned that the pain is natural, valid, and shared by many others. Your sadness is a natural part of grief because of the love you shared with your pet. And it's important to acknowledge and honor these feelings.

We've discovered practical ways to cope with our losses. From creating meaningful tributes to our pets to finding healthy outlets for our emotions, we now have a variety of methods to help us get through and, eventually, out of the hold of grief. Remember, healing is not a linear process—there will be good days and bad days, but with each passing moment, we grow stronger.

Moving on, one of the most important lessons we've learned is why we need to constantly challenge societal stigmas surrounding pet loss. Your grief is real and significant. Don't let anyone diminish your feelings or rush your healing process. Never allow anyone to tell you that your grief, sadness, or lack of drive because of pet loss is unacceptable. Always remember that pet loss and the grief that comes with it are just the same as when we lose people we loved and were close to. Similarly, by openly discussing our experiences and our feelings, we not only heal ourselves but also pave the way for others to seek support without shame. Your journey through grief can help others learn how to battle their demons, come out of the sorrow, and heal.

We've also explored the power of connection. Through shared stories and experiences, we've seen that we're not alone in this journey. There's a whole community of pet lovers who understand your pain and are ready to offer their support. You should never be scared to reach out when you need to; you might be surprised by the comfort you find in shared experiences. Knowing that you're not alone in something can truly help remove some of the weight off your shoulders and offer you some relief.

While the pain of loss may never completely disappear, we've learned that it's possible to find joy again. Your capacity for love hasn't diminished just because the pain is starting to lessen and ease up a bit on your heart; as a matter of fact, it's grown. For this reason, when you're ready, this expanded heart of yours might even let you, or rather encourage you, to welcome a new pet into your home and your heart. And remember: This is not a replacement but a new chapter in your life.

Nearing the close of this book, I would like to thank you for allowing me to be part of your healing journey. I hope this book has provided you with comfort, understanding, and practical tools to go through your grief. Remember, the love you shared with your pet is eternal. It lives on in your memories, in the lessons you learned, and in the person you've become because of that special bond.

Though our paths may diverge, remember that we are never truly alone, for the love of our departed friends goes beyond the boundaries of time and space.

References

Ahn, J.-H., Sang Won Lee, Kim, K., Jin, B. & Un Sun Chung. (2023). The relationship between childhood trauma experience and complicated grief: The importance of psychological support for individuals coping with pet loss in Korea. *Journal of Korean Medical Science, 38*(37). https://doi.org/10.3346/jkms.2023.38.e305

Chakma, S. K., Islam, T. T., Shahjalal, M. & Mitra, D. K. (2021). Depression among pet owners and non-pet owners: a comparative cross-sectional study in Dhaka, Bangladesh. *F1000Research, 10,* 574. https://doi.org/10.12688/f1000research.53276.1

Human-animal bond | American Veterinary Medical Association. (n.d.). Www.avma.org. https://www.avma.org/resources-tools/one-health/human-animal-bond

Johns Hopkins Medicine. (2022). *The friend who keeps you young.* Hopkinsmedicine.org. https://www.hopkinsmedicine.org/health/wellness-and-prevention/the-friend-who-keeps-you-young#:~:text=Research%20has%20shown%20that%20simply

Kübler-Ross, E. (n.d.). *Elisabeth Kübler-Ross.* https://www.siue.edu/counseling/pdf/stages%20of%20grief.pdf

Martins, C., Jorge Pinto Soares, António Cortinhas, Silva, L., Cardoso, L., Pires, M. A. & Maria Paula Mota. (2023). Pet's influence on humans' daily physical activity and mental health: A meta-analysis. *Frontiers in Public Health, 11.* https://doi.org/10.3389/fpubh.2023.1196199

Mughal, S. & Siddiqui, W. J. (2019, March 25). *Grief reaction.* Nih.gov; StatPearls   Publishing. https://www.ncbi.nlm.nih.gov/books/NBK507832/

My experience of losing a pet and what helped my recovery | Anxiety NZ. (n.d.). Anxiety.org.nz.   https://anxiety.org.nz/resources/my-experience-of-losing-a-pet-and-what-helped-my-recovery

Packman, W., Carmack, B. J. & Ronen, R. (2012). Therapeutic implications of continuing bonds expressions following the death of a pet. *OMEGA - Journal of Death and Dying, 64*(4), 335–356. https://doi.org/10.2190/om.64.4.d

Pilgram, M. (2010, September). *Communicating social support to grieving clients: the   veterinarians'   view.*   ResearchGate. https://www.researchgate.net/publication/259990254_Comm unicating_Social_Support_to_Grieving_Clients_The_Veterinari ans'_View

The power of pets: health benefits of human-animal interactions. (2018, February).   NIH. https://newsinhealth.nih.gov/2018/02/power-pets

Robinson, L. & Segal, J. (2019, February 13). *The health and mood-boosting benefits   of   pets.*   HelpGuide.org;   HelpGuide.org. https://www.helpguide.org/articles/mental-health/mood-boosting-power-of-dogs.htm

Uccheddu, S., De Cataldo, L., Albertini, M., Coren, S., Da Graça Pereira, G., Haverbeke, A., Mills, D., Pierantoni, L., Riemer, S., Ronconi, L., Testoni, I. & Pirrone, F. (2019). Pet humanisation and related grief: development and validation of a structured questionnaire instrument to evaluate grief in people who have lost a companion dog. *Animals, 9*(11), 933. https://doi.org/10.3390/ani9110933

WebMD Editorial Contributors. (2024, February 25). *What to know about   repressed   emotions.*   WebMD. https://www.webmd.com/mental-health/what-to-know-repressed-emotions#:~:text=There%20isn

What makes the bond between pet and human so special? (2023, February 27.) Earthpet. https://earthpet.co.za/what-makes-the-bond-between-pet-and-human-so-special/

www.ingramcontent.com/pod-product-compliance
Lightning Source LLC
Chambersburg PA
CBHW020740130626
46554CB00006B/2070